PRAISE

"In his new book, Casey has brought his experience and stories to really drive home what retirement is all about and how to achieve it successfully. This is great food for thought for those approaching retirement."

~Dr. Wade Pfau
Professor of Retirement Income at the American College
Author & Founder of Retirement Researcher

"Casey delivers a very personal and powerful message in his book, *Job Optional*, and continues to move the needle forward for the financial planning profession. This is a must-read for anyone doing retirement income planning."

~Jamie Hopkins
J.D., LL.M., CFP
Director of Retirement Research at Carson Group

"Casey Weade delivers sound wisdom packaged in a fresh, relevant form. Dive into his content and you'll grow yourself as well as your assets."

~Kary Oberbrunner
Speaker, Coach & Author of *Day Job to Dream Job*

"A unique and refreshing take on breaking free from your 9 to 5 and preparing for your dream retirement; not just the financial side, but the emotions that come along with beginning a new chapter and making sure your Golden Years are fulfilling."

~Dr. Hans Finzel
Best-selling Author of *Launch Your Encore*
President of HDLeaders

"A must-read for sound financial guidance. Casey compacts several years' worth of retirement planning experience into an easy-to-follow guide to having the financial freedom to step away from your job and into your next chapter."

~Cody Foster
Co-founder & Owner of Advisors Excel

"Most investment professionals focus strictly on the financial side of retirement planning. But Casey Weade believes retirement planning should start with the question, "What does a purposeful retirement mean to you?" His book will help you create a meaningful retirement that is both financially secure and personally rewarding. Using his advice, the rest of your life really can be the best of your life."

~Nancy Collamer
Author of *Second-Act Careers:
50+ Ways to Profit from Your Passions During Retirement*

These Endorsements, as such term is defined in SEC Rule 206(4)-1, were provided by individuals who are not clients of Howard Bailey Financial, Inc. These individuals were not compensated for these Endorsements, but have pre-existing business relationships with Casey Weade and/or Howard Bailey Financial, Inc. or an affiliate thereof. These relationships may have incentivized these individuals to provide an Endorsement.

UPDATED EDITION

JOB OPTIONAL*

*** The science of retiring with confidence;
the art of living with purpose.**

CASEY WEADE

The opinions expressed in this material represent the current, good-faith views of the author at the time of publication and are provided for limited purposes, are not definitive investment advice and should not be relied on as such. Any investments or strategies referenced herein do not consider the investment objectives, financial situation or particular needs of any specific person. Product suitability must be independently determined for each individual investor. Casey Weade and Howard Bailey Financial Inc. explicitly disclaim any responsibility for product suitability or suitability determinations related to individual investors.

Some of the investment products discussed herein are considered complex investment products. Such products contain unique risks, terms, conditions and fees specific to each offering. Return of principal is not guaranteed above FDIC insurance limits, if applicable, and is and is subject to the creditworthiness of the issuer. You should not purchase an investment product or make an investment recommendation to a customer until you have read the specific offering documentation and understand the specific investment terms and risks of such investment.

Any guarantees described herein are subject to the claims-paying ability of the issuing company.

Investment Advisory Services may be offered through Howard Bailey Securities, LLC, a registered investment adviser. Working with Howard Bailey Securities, LLC, cannot guarantee investment success or that specific financial goals will be achieved.

Copyright © 2019, 2020, 2021 and 2024 by Casey Weade.
All rights reserved. No part of this publication may be reproduced, distributed or transmitted in any form or by any means, including photocopying, recording or other electronic or mechanical methods, without the prior written permission of the publisher, except in the case of brief quotations embodied in critical reviews and certain other noncommercial uses permitted by copyright law. For permission requests, write to the publisher at the address below.

"Job Optional*," "Retire With Purpose™" and "Howard Bailey Financial" are registered trademarks of Howard Bailey Financial. All rights reserved.

Job Optional* appeared on the Wall Street Journal eBook Best Sellers list from August 9-15, 2019. Job Optional was a #1 Amazon best seller in Retirement Planning on 7/2/19, and a Wall Street Journal eBook Best Seller on 8/9/19.

Casey Weade/Howard Bailey Financial™
5916 Covington Rd. Fort Wayne, IN 46804
www.HowardBailey.com
*Job Optional** Casey Weade—3rd ed.
ISBN: 978-1-962988-20-9

062024

I would like to dedicate this book to my wife and rock, Chelsie,
and my children, Calvin, Carver and Chloe,
who are my greatest purpose in life.

CONTENTS

A Note From the Author	viii
INTRODUCTION Not Your Typical Money Book	1
CHAPTER ONE Basic Lessons Learned From the Greatest Generation	3
CHAPTER TWO Purpose-Based Asset Allocation	29
CHAPTER THREE Liquidity Planning	53
CHAPTER FOUR Income Planning	59
CHAPTER FIVE Flexibility Planning	101
CHAPTER SIX Estate Planning	125
CHAPTER SEVEN Closing	161
Acknowledgments	187
Who is Howard Bailey?	189
A Background on Howard Bailey	191
Endnotes	193

A NOTE FROM THE AUTHOR

I have had the opportunity to work with some amazing clients over the years and have developed wonderful and long-term relationships with many of them. Not only do I appreciate the opportunity to work with them, but I value the trust I have developed with them.

The people whose financial lives are discussed in this book are a composite of many clients I have worked with over the years. As you might expect, the names, situations and personal details shared throughout the book have been changed to protect their privacy.

INTRODUCTION

NOT YOUR TYPICAL MONEY BOOK

This isn't your typical financial book looking to sell you on a product or service; it's unfiltered and candid advice offering actionable items to implement in your personal and financial life. This book is a guide to help you pursue the retirement you have always dreamed of.

This book is about discovering and deciding what your life's purpose is and how to live it to the fullest in "retirement" in whatever way you define it to elevate the meaning you experience every single day.

For you, retirement may mean that you stop working and enjoy each day without the worry of how you will pay for everything.

Or perhaps, for you, retirement means the freedom to quit your current job at a moment's notice with financial confidence and live out your passions.

Or maybe you never want to stop working, and, for you, retiring simply means being able to fund your professional passions without sacrificing your personal endeavors.

Whatever retirement means to you, if you're ready to take the planning of it seriously, you've found the right place to start. We are about to take a deep dive into retirement planning, covering a broad range of topics, risks, ideas and strategies—no holds barred. To have a truly confident retirement, you might have to do some legwork and dig deep.

There is no silver bullet for your retirement years, despite what you may have been told. There are no perfect investments (or plans, for that matter), but if you can identify the specific purpose for your life savings, you can find the most efficient way of getting there.

Once you have a solid understanding of the risks you will face and an outline of the specific strategies to overcome each risk, you can let go of what's next and start living your life in the present, where life is actually happening.

CHAPTER ONE

BASIC LESSONS LEARNED FROM THE GREATEST GENERATION

I remember it like it was yesterday. I was eight years old, sitting in my grandparents' living room in the small town of Ligonier, Indiana, on a Saturday afternoon. My grandparents lived in a modest home on Second Street, just a few blocks from the city park where my dad played as a child. Usually, when I remember the times I spent at my grandparents' home, I remember them sitting around the dining room table playing cards or reading the paper. This Saturday was no different. My grandfather, Howard, was reading the newspaper and my grandmother, Christine, was playing solitaire with actual playing cards (at the time, I didn't even know it was possible to play that game without a computer). I sat in the living room playing with my favorite toy, an old wooden train set that was handed down from a prior generation. I had trouble putting this train set down for anything, much like my own son would in the future—by the scale of the tantrums he would throw, you'd think it was the end of the world when it was time to put down old Thomas the Train. But this afternoon, something was different. I heard a noise we don't hear too often anymore—one that excites most children (and, I think, anyone with an inner child).

What could it be, this tinkling noise I heard passing through the neighborhood of Second Street? You may have already guessed; it was the ice cream man, bearing a truck loaded with any number of frozen treats to delight neighborhood children. As soon as I heard the noise, I jumped out of my seat, knocking my favorite train right off the tracks, and ran to the back of the house. Everyone has a favorite item from the ice cream man, and mine was a red, white and blue Bomb Pop. I knew exactly what I wanted; there was only one problem. Like many eight-year-olds, I was a bit short on money. But I knew where to get some.

I burst past my grandparents, where they serenely sat in the dining room, as I rushed to the back of the house and dove into the closet in my grandparents' bedroom. On my knees, I thrust boots and old books out of the way until BINGO! I'd found it—my grandfather's precious coin collection. My grandfather was an avid coin collector. He had old steel pennies, silver dollars, buffalo nickels—all kinds of good stuff that, to my young mind, wasn't getting any good use just sitting in the back of a musty closet. I grabbed one of his old, tattered coin books, knocked out a handful of precious Bomb Pop-buying coins and ran to the front door as fast as I could. I had been too slow to catch the ice cream man before, and that was not going to happen today!

Before I could even grasp the handle to scoot over the threshold, my grandfather had his hand on my arm with alarm in his eyes. I missed the ice cream man that day, as well as the red, white and blue Bomb Pop that I had lusted after. Yet, what I did get from that day was something much more valuable.

That sunny day was my first real lesson about money—one that would stick with me and shape my life for decades to come.

I've found we all have a memory like this one: an experience that shapes the way we treat our finances, our business or our relationships for the rest of our lives. Psychologists say these memories often come from traumatic experiences as children—usually between five and ten. They may come in the form of an alcoholic father, a drug-addicted mother, bankruptcy, homelessness or death. They can, of course, also be positive experiences. In my case, to my child's mind, I thought missing out on my Bomb Pop was pretty traumatic, but looking back, it's easily recognizable as an overwhelmingly positive lesson.

LESSONS I'VE LEARNED

My Lesson: The Value of a Dollar

My grandfather shared with me many things I didn't understand at that moment. For one, he addressed my feelings about using fifty cents to buy my favorite popsicle. My thought, of course, was, "Why not? It's just sitting there not doing anything at all, and we have the opportunity to turn it into something delicious for immediate enjoyment!" My grandfather very seriously said, "When I was a boy, we didn't have two nickels to rub together, let alone fifty cents to buy a popsicle." My grandfather was a member of "the Greatest Generation," born just a few years before the Great Depression. His parents lost nearly everything, and his earliest memories were formed watching them struggle to put food on the table. This created a great deal of skepticism and conservativism in my grandfather.

My Grandfather's Lesson: Savings Over Investment

I also learned that the Great Depression was responsible for another "quirk" I couldn't understand about my grandparents—something they would often eat called "coffee soup." I've found many different names for this meal (if you want to call it that) over the years. It was a piece of Sunbeam White Bread—none of this suburban whole grain stuff—topped with brown sugar and drowned in a cup of coffee. I couldn't understand why anyone would subject themselves to such torture, but my grandparents ate it fairly regularly. Why? Because it was born out of the experiences they had when they were between the ages of five and ten, setting patterns that, in many ways, were the blueprint for how they would treat their finances for the rest of their lives.

My grandfather was a carpet layer by trade, and my grandmother worked in a local factory. They didn't make a lot of money, but what they made, they saved. They saved it in the local federal credit union, where they knew it was safe. Unfortunately, there was a major embezzlement at this banking institution before credit unions carried NCUA coverage, which was much like the FDIC insurance you are probably more familiar with. When the scandal broke, my dad was at that impressionable age between five and ten. Watching his parents during the ensuing financial hardships of rebuilding their lost savings led him to lean in on that financially conservative nature as well.

These stories, imparted in lieu of a much-coveted Bomb Pop, shaped my way of thinking about saving, spending and investing as a child, but what happened later created the foundation from which I teach finance today. In 2005, my grandfather passed away at age seventy-eight. At the time, I was studying finance in college, learning about the miracles of the stock market and investing in ways my grandfather would never have considered flirting with. When he passed away, it was hard on my family, but the emotional toll was greatest on my grandmother, who was left to pick up the pieces.

My Grandmother's Lesson: Never Lose Money

You see, though my grandmother had the support of my father (who was a financial advisor at the time) as well as my plucky young self, my grandfather did not make his passing easy on her due to his conservative and rather stubborn nature. He did very little in the way of estate planning to help ensure a smooth transition, and, perhaps more vexing, we had our work cut out for us in determining just where their money was in the first place. Sure, there were bank accounts, fixed annuities, certificates of deposit, etc., but there was also a significant amount of money hidden within the house they lived in on Second Street itself. Every visit became an opportunity to find more cash—not just the coin collection my grandfather left behind, but cold, hard cash.

One day, I was cleaning through the small hallway pantry when I discovered an old Maxwell House Coffee can that had obviously been there forever, covered in rust. I reached back, opened the can and found several thousand dollars in rolled-up bills. You see, my grandparents didn't invest like we are told we must invest today to be successful. Raised in the aftermath of a massive stock market crash, they would never imagine owning a stock, bond or mutual fund.

With the experiences my grandfather had with the stock market and the FCU later down the road, he would never risk losing a dime of his hard-earned money.

Make no mistake, it was hard-earned. I often hear people complain about how they don't make enough money to ever retire—either their company doesn't offer a pension or their Social Security benefits just won't be enough. My grandparents never saw a six-figure income and never made a 10 percent return on their investments; they just worked hard and saved. Most importantly, they followed Warren Buffett's Number One Rule of Investing: "Never Lose Money," and they never overlooked Rule Number Two: "Never Forget Rule Number One." They also followed Dave Ramsey's common-sense approach to finance (build an emergency fund, get out of debt and stay there, etc.) before Dave was even a twinkle in his mother's eye. They retired in their sixties and enjoyed a wonderful retirement on a pittance of a pension and little-to-no Social Security income.

When my grandmother passed away in 2013, it was the most painful loss of a loved one I had ever endured. I was incredibly close to her; she taught me not just about responsibility, but, most importantly, she showed me how to enjoy life to the fullest, not to take it too seriously and to always remember to laugh, no matter the situation. When she passed away, I may have learned an even more important lesson that I hope to pass on to anyone reading. Believe it or not, this penny-pinching retired factory worker left behind over a million dollars to my dad and his sister. My mind was blown. Everything I learned in college and all I was taught while completing my boards in pursuit of becoming a CERTIFIED FINANCIAL PLANNER™ practitioner went out the window.

The Great Recession Lesson: Be Cautious and Conservative

In my opinion, over the last few decades, we have slowly lost touch with this way of treating our finances. We have been brainwashed by the mammoth financial industry today into thinking we need to take on significant risks, both in the way of investing and approaching debt, to be successful. This mindset, I might add, was proliferated in the '80s and '90s, when most of today's financial advisors got their start in this business.

Prior to 1974, we didn't have things like 401(k)s. Instead, many relied on the pension plans of the companies they worked for to provide their future retirement, with a golden watch to boot. In 1974, the Employee Retirement Income Security Act (also known as ERISA) was passed, introducing 401(k)s to the masses. Now, the largest generation in history could take money out of their paycheck and invest it directly in the stock market.

On top of this, the advent of the internet led to the first internet brokerage firm in August 1994: K. Aufhauser & Company, Inc., later acquired by TD Ameritrade. Brokerage firms popped up on every street corner and in every shopping mall to help us get a piece of the biggest bull market in history. If you think about it, stock market investing for the masses has only been around for a short period of time. Throughout the early 2000s, investors were smacked with reality twice as the market lost half of its value. It was during this period that I began practicing in the investing and financial world as part of what will be known as "the Great Recession Generation," continuing the cautious and conservative nature of previous generations in my family.

My Dad's Lesson: Don't Get Overconfident; Stocks Aren't for Everyone

My dad wasn't without financial turmoil in his own life, which lent itself to many learning opportunities for me, in addition to the lessons I learned from my grandparents. Much of my parents' wealth was made in their real estate investing escapades. In an unfortunate series of events, we watched as most of it crumbled during the 2008 financial crisis and real estate bubble.

It wasn't always that way, of course. As a kid, I remember living in a small apartment, but by the mid-'90s, Dad had purchased his own apartment complex made up of forty units. This became like a family farm to us. My dad and grandfather laid carpet on the weekends, my mother balanced the books and cleaned after renters moved out, my other grandfather (Ralph) helped get new renters their keys and I often spent weekends keeping the grounds clean and picking up the trash that seemed to have so much trouble hitting the dumpsters. If you've ever owned rentals, then you know the property management side of the business is not for the lazy. My dad took a loan out for the purchase of the property, later paying it off with the sale of the property just after the tech crash of the 2000s.

In the '80s, my father started a second career as a financial advisor. I remember asking my mom if Dad could come outside and play, but he was busy studying for his securities license at the time. Like many people, he wholeheartedly bought into the booming stock market and the opportunities it offered. Not only did he place his IRAs and his non-real estate investments in mutual funds, but he would also often pressure my grandfather to do the same. I remember sitting around the dining room table eating supper at my grandparents' while my dad would pull out his personal investment statements, brag about his returns and flaunt them to my grandfather, trying to show him what his money should be doing. Meanwhile, my grandfather would grumble, stuck in his ways, saying, "It'll all come crashing down, you'll see!" Well, he was right; the tech bubble peaked on March 10, 2000.

Shortly after, we saw the terrorist attacks of September 11, 2001, drag the market down even further. My father lost more than half his life's savings in three short years. I can remember him sitting in his home office every day, logging into his brokerage account and just trying to get back to even. You see, while the stock market may have only been down around 40 percent, many investors lost substantially more due to the over-weighted tech sector in many mutual funds. It took him years to make up his losses; he recovered right in time for the financial crisis of 2008.

Luckily, by that time, Dad had decided the stock market wasn't for him. When he experienced the losses of 2000-2003 firsthand, he had just sold his apartment complex. He couldn't imagine enduring the kind of losses he had experienced in his other investments without the cash from the sale of what was probably the best investment he ever made. Not only was it one of the best investments he had ever made, but he saw it as a family investment. Blood, sweat and tears of multiple generations went into those apartments, and Dad wouldn't be able to stand losing a dime.

On a related note, I find this to be very true for self-created wealth—whether it is an entrepreneurial business, farm or other real estate investment, most of these individuals who have worked to build something don't want to risk their life savings or the blood, sweat and tears of multiple generations. Contrast this to the average 401(k) investor who built most of their wealth by piling money into the mutual funds in their employer's retirement plan. The latter individuals are often more comfortable with the extreme volatility seen in the public markets.

Why is this an important point? When I meet with entrepreneurs (farmers, real estate moguls, business owners, etc.), I find they can typically relate to not wanting to risk their life savings. By having a stronger connection to their money, they usually make smarter, more conservative decisions that lead to longer-term success as opposed to those who just watched their 401(k)s ebb and flow.

From those days forward, Dad put his money almost exclusively into fixed income and real estate investments; he was never going back to a market that could wash away half of his wealth overnight. This mentality of protection and conservativism would continue into another generation.

The Common "Cents" of Generations Past

In large part, I feel we have lost touch with the common sense and conservative approach of past generations. Instead, we've been trained to seek get-rich-quick schemes, big returns, the next best investment or the silver bullet that will make us wealthy overnight. I'm here to tell you these things don't exist. There are those who have hit the home run in the lottery or with lucky investments, but they could have just as easily struck out.

Striking out in retirement isn't where you want to end up. Whether you have taken market risks with your 401(k) to accumulate your wealth, owned a business that could have ended at any time due to the unknown or taken on debt to finance real estate that could have defaulted—no matter how you made it, you've made it. You've made it to the glory land called retirement. It's time to preserve your wealth and make it last a lifetime. It's time to look back on the Greatest Generation and take a page from their book. This all starts with deciding what you want out of retirement in the first place. Congratulations on your Job Optional status.

The Definition of Retirement

You may be wondering, "When are we going to get to the financial advice and investment recommendations?" The reality is that while most financial advisors start there, it should really be where you finish. I've seen far too many retirees quit working only to be lost in the day-to-day monotony of retirement. I learned this firsthand as I watched my father try and fail at his own retirement by doing just that.

To Work or Not to Work?

Without a higher purpose or calling in his life, Dad floundered. He gave up golf after the yips made a 6-foot putt an adventure. He then decided, rather quickly, that he was happier working. He launched a new career as a financial advisor after just a couple of short years of retirement.

As I write this book, Dad is beginning to prepare for his second attempt at retirement. He has found a passion for travel and helping others enjoy their travel to the fullest. Not only that, but he has a couple of grandkids to help him make up for any lost time we missed when I was a kid. Forty hours was a part-time job when I was little, and, as a result, I spent most of my time between my mother and grandparents. Now, Dad has a second chance at retirement and has found a purpose for all his free time—it will be time well spent with family and pursuing his new passions.

TRUTH:
IT'S NOT THE SIZE OF YOUR BANK ACCOUNT.

FROM THOUSANDAIRES TO BILLIONAIRES, PEOPLE FIND TRUE HAPPINESS BY FINDING AND FULFILLING THEIR PURPOSE IN LIFE.

My father is in the perfect place I call Job Optional. He can now choose to work or not work, to keep building his career contributions, fulfill personal passions or both. He is in control. He is an example of the science behind retiring and the art of Retiring with Purpose.

What Does It Mean to Retire With Purpose™?

After working one-on-one with thousands of people planning for retirement, I can tell you without hesitation that this planning must start with a purpose. Successful retirement planning is all about a purposeful life.

So, what do I mean when I say "purposeful life?" Here are a few real-life examples of people who retired with purpose and how it impacted them.

Retired with Purpose: Patrick and Brenda Their Purpose: "Creating the marriage we never could."

One of the happiest couples I have ever worked with, leading one of the most fulfilling retirements I have ever seen, isn't the wealthiest in savings but is by far the wealthiest in life. Patrick and Brenda, who were working as an engineer and a nurse, looked forward to retiring with a few hundred thousand dollars and a pension, but they were not the happiest people when we first met. During our initial visit, they never broke a smile.

They often discussed their pessimistic outlook on the economy and focused on how politics could put their future and that of their children in jeopardy. Up until then, their careers consisted of working competing hours, raising four children and missing out on what they described as "a lifetime with one another." They had never seen the Grand Tetons, Glacier National Park or even Nashville, for that matter.

While they were true pessimists, they were crystal clear about what they wanted for their retirement. Their purpose in finalizing a retirement strategy was to simply start over by building the life they always wanted but never had.

After we had finalized their retirement plans, the first thing they did was renew their vows and set out on the honeymoon they had never taken. They ultimately purchased an RV, got a new dog and began traveling the country, essentially starting over with the purpose of creating—in their words—"the marriage we could never have."

They now attend all our private client events and quarterly reviews with the biggest smiles of any clients I have ever worked with, often saying they are happier than they have ever been.

Prior to implementing their very own Retire With Purpose™ Framework, they worried about all the unknown risks they faced in retirement and how it could all be over in the blink of an eye. Once we laid out the major risks they would face in retirement and, more importantly, structured a plan to address each one systematically, they said those worries went away. By having a plan for the worst-case scenario, they could turn off the news channels and move on with life on their own terms, no longer having to worry about what's next.

Now, everyone is different. For you, waiting until retirement to really begin living your dream life may be your preference. Or maybe for you, retiring is just a second act.

Retired with Purpose: My Mentor His Purpose: "To be and create."

Years ago, I was introduced to a business owner who had started his business in the family barn, growing it to a $100 million company.

Being part of the advisory team for the sale of that company was one of the most fulfilling and exciting experiences I have ever had as an advisor. Seeing someone start something from scratch, change hundreds of lives and influence global retail in the process was inspiring. We spent dozens of hours together prior to the sale of the business, discussing purpose, meaning and what the next stage of life would look like. Along the way, he helped me discover my purpose in life and in business, becoming one of my closest friends and mentors. After the sale of the business, he decided to pursue starting a new business from the ground up, which he felt had the potential to change the world. He had never had the time or resources to devote to his new endeavor until he "retired." Now, he spends most of his time building an even more influential company and fulfilling his purpose, which he stated is "to be and create." He could do this because he had his Retire With Purpose™ Framework to fall back on, allowing him to focus on his true purpose for this next stage of his life and put the worries of "money" behind him. His story is unique in terms of the scale of his projects, but I have seen many retirees with this same mentality.

Typically, they are highly driven entrepreneurs and thinkers; these individuals almost shouldn't retire in the traditional sense, as it would be a shock to their system. For many of these gifted men and women, "retiring" from creating, inventing and using their God-given gifts to change the world for the better would truly be a loss to society. Not everyone has these talents, but if you do, don't squander them, or you will eventually look back with regret!

For these movers and shakers, this is not a reason to ignore retirement planning—the financial realities of retirement are ultimately impossible to avoid. On the contrary, if you have a retirement plan to fall back on, then you can take bigger risks in following the new dreams you long to fulfill—dreams you may not have been able to pursue during your working career. This may not be as big as starting a whole new career. It may be as simple as part-time or contract work in the previous career you are familiar with because you still have so much to offer.

My own sense of purpose became crystal clear during one of the most challenging times of my life. In 2017, our second son, Carver, was born with a rare congenital defect known as Congenital Diaphragmatic Hernia (CDH). This occurs when the diaphragm of the child fails to close during prenatal development. We were told the best way to give Carver a chance at survival would be to relocate his birth and care to the Cincinnati Children's Hospital, where the only team specializing in CDH existed in the world. This required our family to move temporarily to Cincinnati for six months, and that ended up being my greatest chapter of clarity.

At the time, I had never taken more than a week away from my work. It was a "forced retirement," in a sense. I spent this time contemplating my future and what was most important to me in life. I did what I thought I was supposed to do, which was focusing all of my energy on my family, health and faith.

Given that my sole focus up until this point in life was on building a successful business, a reprioritization felt in order. Within several weeks, I was borderline depressed. I realized these were the same feelings that so many retirees experience. For decades, they prioritize the accumulation of wealth, often spending less time focusing on the most important aspects of life (family, health, faith, etc.). When they finally reach financial independence, many might find themselves unhappy after achieving exactly what they worked so hard for. Why?

It's because there is an element missing from the fulfillment equation that goes beyond family, health and faith: contribution. Contribution is about others. It's the shared purpose we all have in helping others, and we leverage our God-given talents for that contribution.

I realized I was gifted at helping others identify what they really want in life. Then, I would help design a strategy and coach them toward their dream. Now, much like where you may find yourself today, I have the time and ability to leverage my financial freedom to create more balance in my life. I focus my God-given talents on areas where I can make the biggest contribution: deriving a greater sense of purpose through impact.

I'm happy, and you deserve to be, too. You can find fulfillment by intentionally leveraging your blessings to help others. Now, am I retired? Of course not—not in the traditional sense, at least. I consider myself to be Job Optional, and I'm doing what I want to do every day. That's what retirement is really all about, isn't it?

Retired with Purpose: Ralph Bailey His Purpose: "Helping students, teachers and educational leaders throughout the state."

My maternal grandfather, Ralph Bailey, was one of those individuals. My grandfather became the school principal of Etna-Troy, a school for grades one through eight, at the age of twenty-five. He later became a superintendent of schools. He eventually became one of the most influential people in the educational system in Indiana, helping to shape the political world of education for years to come. The state recognized him with the Sagamore of the Wabash, an award for his work in education. At the time, it was the highest honor the governor of Indiana could bestow as a personal tribute, usually given to those who provided distinguished service to the state or to the governor.

When I called to wish my grandfather a happy eighty-sixth birthday, he told me he had just been offered a three-year extension on his contract as superintendent of Smith-Green Community Schools, a local school corporation. In his nineties, my grandfather still began every morning by putting on a suit and going to work to manage a full schedule, helping students, teachers and educational leaders throughout the state. All the while, he had a retirement plan; he didn't need to work, but he continued fulfilling a higher purpose, which helped to keep him as one of the sharpest ninety-somethings I have ever met.

Not all retirees choose traveling, starting a new career or consulting to fulfill their purpose. Some are more spiritual quests.

Retired with Purpose: Rick and Jeannette Their Purpose: "Starting their own church in a small town."

One couple I worked with, Rick and Jeannette, spent their careers traveling the country, climbing the corporate ladder from one Fortune 500 CFO position to the next. They were referred to me by another client of mine, as they were looking to make a transition to a retirement specialist and local advisor before their move back home to Indiana from Texas. Our visits together were almost entirely online since Rick would work long hours at his job out of state.

Despite the corporate expense account and every trapping of power, Rick was a humble man with humble goals, and our conversations often focused on his and Jeannette's purpose in retirement and what they wanted their money to accomplish for them. Rick often lamented that Jeannette, who had retired, spent her time flying out to spend time with their grandchildren while he felt trapped at work, stuck doing something he didn't enjoy and offered no challenge.

While the company had presented him with the prospect of making more income than he could ever imagine if he stayed, you could feel

Rick's angst, as he knew it just wasn't that important anymore. Staying meant earning money he and Jeannette would never be able to spend while forgoing some of the most meaningful experiences of his life. They had a dream of starting their own church in a small town just outside of Huntington, Indiana. They had saved multiple millions of dollars throughout his working career and weren't big spenders. After helping to build and examine their budget, they needed less than $100,000 per year in after-tax income to live the life they were accustomed to. They had nearly $70,000 per year in pension and Social Security benefits even before they factored in the millions of savings. The quick math said they had way more than they needed. This lent itself to a grand discussion regarding risk, as he was one whom many would regard as having more than enough to afford to take on substantial risk with his retirement for greater growth opportunities. However, he said to me, "Casey, why would we take the risk if we don't need to? If we just preserve what we have and don't lose it, we will have enough money to last for the rest of our lives without worries."

There is a great lesson to be learned here, as even though Rick had been trained to take risks his entire working life to be successful, he recognized he had "made it," and he didn't want to worry about it anymore. By structuring our proprietary Retire With PurposeTM Framework (we will get to that in detail shortly) to focus on preserving their life savings, Rick and Jeannette could focus on the more important things in their life—like spending more time in the church and with family—rather than what stock they should pick next.

Retired with Purpose: The Doctor His Purpose: "Give away time and expertise to those in need."

Another gentleman I worked with was a physician who felt frustrated with what he saw in a money-driven medical community and set out to give his time and experience away to those in need all over the world. As he finally made his transition into retirement, he often asked why he didn't start sooner. He always felt he didn't have enough money to retire and was making too much to quit. The reality was that he had created enough wealth to last the rest of his life years prior to our first meeting, but he never sat down and really examined his retirement to determine what was possible. As a result, he lost time he will never get back, but now that he has a plan that will allow him to move on to fulfill his purpose, he says he'll never look back. He spends his time giving back to the world and serves on boards to positively impact change in the medical community. Whatever you decide doesn't have to be grandiose, but without thinking, you will look back at some point in your life with regret, wondering what would have been possible if you had just taken the time to plan and reflect.

How to Start Practicing for Retirement

One of the best ways for you to start this journey is to practice your retirement. Envision what you will do and how you will spend your days. This can start with simply planning out what you might want a day in retirement to look like.

- What time do you wake up? Where do you have breakfast?
- Who do you spend your time with throughout the day?
- What time do you have dinner and where?
- What time do you go to bed?

Playing out a full day of retirement is just the start, then you can take the next step to envision your month-to-month and year-to-year plans.

When interviewing Nancy Collamer, author of *Second-Act Careers: 50+ Ways to Profit from Your Passions During Semi-Retirement*, for the

Retire With Purpose™ podcast, she walked through how she coaches pre-retirees to outline their "ideal" day in retirement and how to create the "ideal" year in retirement. I especially enjoyed the word "ideal," as it's one thing to envision just another day in retirement, but a perfect day helps deepen your perspective. I prefer to walk our clients through first identifying a typical day and then using that foundation to begin making edits to envision what an "ideal" or perfect day would look like.

Identify the gaps in your time and how you will fill them. Going from full speed to a dead stop can cause significant trauma, so prepare yourself for what your life might be like. This is the start of creating your very own Retire With Purpose™ Framework. After you have identified your purpose, then—and only then—can you set out to organize your assets in such a way to most efficiently accomplish that purpose and elevate your sense of meaning in life.

Retired with Purpose: YOU? Your Purpose: What drives you?

Have you thought about what makes you tick? What gets you passionate? What do you want to dedicate your time, energy and money to outside of your career? Have you considered how important working is to you? How would you feel if you no longer worked day to day?

One of the challenges I face when working with new clients is identifying the answers to these questions. The reason is that what motivates people is deeply personal and individual.

There was a study conducted in 2000 called the Cornell Retirement and Well-Being Study, which concluded that about 44 percent of retirees worked for pay after their retirement began. Did they need the money? Were they bored? Why take a job after retiring from the workforce? The answers are in what drives you personally.

The study went on to detail that, of those currently employed after retirement, 14 percent say they will "never retire," and 28 percent say they will work "as long as I am healthy." Most want their time to be filled with personal passions and new experiences.

Other reasons for returning to work after retiring:

- Have free time – 73 percent
- Desire additional income – 63 percent
- Not ready to retire – 58 percent
- Maintain social contacts – 56 percent

Discovering Your Motivation Is Important in Retiring With Purpose™

When considering your Job Optional status and your Retire With Purpose™ Framework, you have to determine what motivates you. There are dozens of motivating factors. Here are a few of my favorites to consider when thinking about your purpose and how your financial confidence fits into that purpose.

#1.	Accomplishments – to collect experiences
#2.	Action – to stay relevant and active
#3.	Authority – to be a leader and contributor
#4.	Belonging – to feel a part of something bigger
#5.	Creativity – to express your artistic side
#6.	Friendship – to stay connected to a social circle
#7.	Identity – to feel like yourself through actions
#8.	Intellectual Stimulation – to keep your brain engaged
#9.	Lifelong Learning – to continue to develop new skills
#10.	Making a Difference – to leave a legacy and impact
#11.	Mentoring – to pass on your knowledge to others
#12.	Passion – to engage in what makes you feel most alive

#13.   Problem Solving – to contribute to a solution

#14.   Self-Esteem – to feel good through contribution

#15.   Value – to provide value to others and feel valued

Patrick and Michelle designed their Framework around #12 – Passion and #4 – Belonging by committing to a new life that brought them closer together through their shared passions.

My mentor designed his Framework around #3 – Authority, #11 – Mentoring and #15 – Value by creating a second career not based on needing money but on providing support and education to people who motivated him.

Ralph Bailey designed his Framework around #1 – Accomplishments, #7 – Identity and #10 – Making a Difference, working to inspire others until his final days. That was my grandfather's legacy.

Rick and Jeannette designed their Framework around #4 – Belonging and #7 – Identity by creating connections with others through the things they felt the most connected to in life.

The doctor designed his Framework around #2 – Action, #8 – Intellectual Stimulation and #10 – Making a Difference by passing on his skills and knowledge so that he had the greatest impact in his field of reach.

When you meet with traditional financial planners, you often come away with cut-and-dry plans to move your money around in ways that simply mitigate risk in retirement or improve the potential for better returns. There is not a lot of consideration for what you will do in retirement. You could argue that helping someone retire financially could be a disservice if that retiree will then feel listless and unfulfilled.

BASIC LESSONS LEARNED FROM THE GREATEST GENERATION

Certainly, most financial planners are not starting with the big purpose questions:

1. Do you want to stop working altogether or work on your own terms?
2. What day-to-day activities will make you happy and fulfilled in retirement?
3. Are you clear on the legacy you want your life savings to leave?

When I talk to clients about retirement, I always start with purpose first. It is important to remember that the motivation behind your purpose is not your activities or actions. Motivation is what personally drives you. Your motivations are unique and personal to you. Your purpose is intimately linked to these motivating drivers. Think of your motivation as internal and your purpose as external. Your internal motivation drives your external actions or purpose. When you can identify what motivates you, then planning for your retirement becomes less scary.

A confident retirement starts with true education about your risks and options to mitigate them so you don't have to worry about what's around the corner next year. Preparing your finances (properly) for retirement is one of those things that is simple but not easy— some of the biggest threats to our retirement confidence come from an emotional place, not necessarily a rational one.

When you begin planning for retirement with purpose and clearly identifiable motives, then organizing the four key factors in retirement becomes much easier.

People are increasingly able to retire younger and younger, and the options they have after retirement are now greater and greater. This is why *Job Optional** seemed like the perfect title for this book—with clear purpose and proper planning, the choice in how, when and why you "retire" is yours.

JOB OPTIONAL

TAKEAWAYS, ACTIONS AND NOTES

What are your biggest takeaways from this chapter?

_____

_____

_____

_____

_____

_____

_____

What are three action steps that you should work on now?

1. _____

2. _____

3. _____

What are three action steps for later?

1. _____

2. _____

3. _____

BASIC LESSONS LEARNED FROM THE GREATEST GENERATION

NOTES:

CHAPTER TWO

PURPOSE-BASED ASSET ALLOCATION

Investing is a big factor when it comes to retirement, and many pre-retirees and retirees hyper-focus on it. It is my belief that you must look beyond investing and into areas such as higher taxes, gaps in health care coverage and inflation—these are the inefficiencies that, if left untreated, can drain your assets and leave fewer dollars in your pocket and that of your heirs.

I refer to this as Purpose-Based Asset Allocation.[1]

Most of the time, meeting with a financial advisor is like running into a local pharmacy to fix a cold. You're prescribed an over-the-counter medication after a ten-minute consultation without regard to the real problem. Now, if it's just a cold, maybe your quick visit fixed your issue, but when it comes to your retirement, we're not facing a minor illness but instead a major ailment with many accompanying risks.

Your financial doctor will need to make significant preparations, just as you may take for knee surgery or something as serious as heart surgery.

Before my wife had knee surgery, we had several consultations with general practitioners and specialists. They didn't just prescribe the knee surgery but took their time to identify the issue and the ultimate treatment. They even took her blood pressure and heart rate, which you may think are unrelated, but the potential risks from not checking these things, as well as medical history, could result in death.

I would argue that the same is true for your retirement planning. The risks are broad, and without taking into consideration all factors, you could overlook something, putting your financial health at risk. Real financial planning takes everything into account before any "medications" are ultimately prescribed. This is not only going to allow your planner to recommend the most appropriate strategies for your retirement but will also allow you to understand why they are making those recommendations in the first place. I find that the better we understand the rationale behind a decision, the more confident we are that we have made a good one, and, as a result, this allows us to live a more confident retirement.

Do You Know Where Your Money Is?

Many retirees just have a pile of money invested in various ways they don't understand. I met some who have multiple advisors and dozens of accounts—many working against one another.

PURPOSE-BASED ASSET ALLOCATION

MEET DENNIS AND KAREN

Years ago, I met the sweetest couple, Dennis and Karen, who were truly hard workers, not only in their careers but in their personal lives, as well. They had biological children in their younger years, but when they found they couldn't have any more, they set out to adopt. They had planned to adopt a healthy child, but one day Dennis was confronted with a seemingly difficult decision. A special needs baby had come up for adoption. He immediately called Karen and said if they didn't adopt her, then who would? Without skipping a beat, Karen said to bring the baby home, knowing this would be a lifetime commitment and they would be taking care of this child into their golden years. This was just the kind of people they were, some of the hardest working and caring individuals I know. Along the way, they were always focused on how to earn more, cover their expenses and find a little extra to put away for retirement.

However, problems were evident. They would go from one investment to the next as they changed jobs. They had recommendations from friends and met with various advisors over the years. Each presented them with the next shiny object to resolve their financial woes and get them to retirement. And, as busy as they were between their careers and taking care of their children, there was little time left over for planning for retirement.

When I met Dennis and Karen, I walked into the conference room to greet them and saw some of the other chairs in the room were filled with a briefcase and a couple of grocery bags. It turned out the briefcase and those grocery bags were full of investment and insurance statements from all the "shiny objects" they had been sold over the years.

They didn't know how much money they had, where it was or what it was doing for them. They didn't feel they had enough for retirement, and they realized they didn't have a plan. This caused them stress and could have been the cause of various ailments they had suffered over the years.

Dennis and Karen had variable annuities for which they paid fees for benefits they would never use. They had mutual funds with expenses that could have been eliminated years prior. They had life insurance policies for which they were either overpaying or that had convoluted death benefit requirements for which they would likely never qualify. They were paying unnecessary taxes on after-tax investments. They had no beneficiaries listed on many of their accounts, and, perhaps most importantly of all, they had no idea how much money they really had, let alone an estate plan to ensure their special needs daughter would be taken care of after they were gone.

Many of these products and investments were working against each other through "portfolio overlap" and misaligned benefits. It ended up taking us years to uncover all the different places they had stuffed away money. Just about every time they came in to review their assets, they brought in a new statement that had come in the mail from some unexpected and long-forgotten asset.

Once we determined exactly what they had and where it was, we could finally organize it toward their common purpose in retirement. Once Dennis and Karen had cut their unnecessary expenses and aligned their investments with their true goals, they had nearly twice the assets they thought they did and were finally ready to put the financial worries and stress of the rat race behind them. They retired to spend time with their children and previously neglected hobbies; they finally started taking care of themselves the way they should have years prior.

Liability vs. Purpose-Based Planning

How can you have peace of mind without specifically identifying the unique risks your retirement will face and how each one of your assets will address them?

Liability-Driven Planning

The definition of Liability-Driven Planning is when you have already created the asset, and the only things that can take it away are the liabilities you will potentially face. In my experience, along the way, uncertainty regarding the future often leads people to inappropriate investments and unnecessary stresses due to their desire to preserve assets against undefined liabilities.

> THE BIGGEST MISTAKES I HAVE SEEN RETIREES MAKE ARE DUE TO NOT HAVING A PLAN FOR THEIR POTENTIAL RISKS OR LIABILITIES WHEN THEY ARISE, LEADING TO PANIC.

Purposed-Based Planning

Purpose-Based Asset Allocation is defined as the actions taken when you identify the specific risks you will face, assess how each one of these risks will affect you and allocate your assets to most efficiently defend against them, systematically starting with the most important. Most simply, the purpose of your assets is four-fold: liquidity, income, flexibility and estate planning.

We call this your financial L.I.F.E. plan, sandwiched between what drives it, your purpose and the result of this work. Collectively, we refer to this as your Retire With Purpose™ Framework, designed as a living, breathing document to assist you in making good decisions whatever comes next.

Regardless of the planning style, all retirees face unique risks for their unique situations, but most will face four basic risks, to varying degrees, which are all part of L.I.F.E.

1. L=Liquidity. These are funds set aside for emergencies and opportunities. Having six to twelve months of funds set aside and readily available provides financial confidence and peace of mind.
2. I=Income. Regardless of what happens next in the economy or stock market, a rock-solid income plan is about having the confidence to spend, knowing you'll have income no matter how long you live or what happens next in the stock market.
3. F=Flexibility. Assets must be set aside to provide the flexibility to adapt to the unpredictability of life. These assets are most often set aside for long-term growth to adjust to the unknown impact of inflation, other market forces and whatever else life may throw at you.
4. E=Estate. An estate plan helps ensure the assets you have will pass on according to your wishes. Clear objectives can be outlined for what you want to leave behind and how—including wills, trusts and health care.

You will face many risks throughout retirement, requiring specific strategies to address them, including things like:

- Market corrections—maybe even crashes—that jeopardize the reliability of your retirement income
- Longevity risk or the risk of outliving your retirement savings
- Rising taxes that reduce your annual income and the assets you plan to leave behind
- Inflation pressures that reduce the purchasing power of your spendable income
- Major health care expenses that place an undue burden on loved ones

> **YOU WILL FACE UNKNOWN EMERGENCIES DURING RETIREMENT, REQUIRING LIQUIDITY TO FUND THEM.**

Maximizing Your Efficiency

My middle school cross-country coach had a dry demeanor yet was full of wisdom in the little things he said. At every practice and before every meet, he would tell us to remember that the shortest distance between two points was a straight line. In running, that meant staying on the inside track instead of taking the long way around on corners.

In retirement, the same concept applies: inefficiencies in your portfolio may not completely prevent you from achieving your financial goals, but they sure won't help you attain your goals faster.

Many of the retirees we meet with have their entire retirement in a portfolio of mutual funds, which they are relying on to be there for emergencies, satisfy a lifetime of income needs, provide flexibility to adapt to things like inflation, cover any major health care expenses they may incur AND leave a financial legacy to their heirs to boot. As a result, nothing is positioned efficiently. If they incur an emergency while the market is down, they risk selling at a loss. If the market loses substantial value, they risk taking larger withdrawals and running out of money. If they have a major long-term care need, the portfolio could be drained and leave nothing to their heirs.

> A mutual fund is an investment vehicle that is made up of a pool of funds collected from many investors for the purpose of investing in securities such as stocks, bonds, money market instruments and similar assets. Mutual funds are operated by money managers who invest the fund's capital and attempt to produce capital gains and income for the fund's investors.

A gentleman who visited with our team reflected a product-specific example of an inefficient retirement plan. He had all his retirement savings invested in a variable annuity from a policy purchased years prior. He wanted out of the annuity but could not exit, in his mind, because of a large death benefit rider on the policy. When we evaluated the cost of the death benefit rider, we found we could pay the same premium to a life insurance carrier and get a substantially larger tax-free death benefit than he would get as a taxable death benefit in his annuity. In addition, we could reposition the funds inside the annuity into an investment portfolio that would cut his fees and expenses in half, unleashing the growth power of his savings. Unleashing the efficiency of your life savings requires you to identify the specific purpose AND have the right tools in place to accomplish it.

Identifying Risks to Maximize Efficiency

Retirees have always faced the same general risks. However, these risks have evolved over time, and so must your strategies; otherwise, it's akin to driving down the highway while looking in the rearview mirror.

I was once given a pointer about keeping the future in focus: "You must recognize there is a reason your front windshield is bigger than the rearview mirror—the most important part of preparing for the future is recognizing that it lies in front of you."

Risk 1: Interest Rates

Depending on your age, you may have a different reaction to the concept of "interest rates." Chances are, if you are reading this book and preparing for retirement, you'll recall the rate of return you could get on a certificate of deposit (CD) back in the 1980s or even just ten or twenty years ago. In 1981, the peak of interest rates in modern history, even a three-month CD could pay about 18 percent interest. As recently as 2002, my dad purchased a fixed annuity that paid a guaranteed 7 percent interest annually for ten years.[2]

If you could get a 7 percent guaranteed interest rate, odds are you wouldn't be reading this book. Higher guaranteed interest rates could solve a multitude of risks you will face in retirement—granted, they wouldn't solve all your risks, as you would still face such things as taxes and health care expenses. Still, normalizing interest rates would greatly improve your financial efficiency overall.

Stocks, bonds and cash used to be the foundation of all financial strategies. Many unfortunate investors who thought their fixed-income holdings would safeguard them against market downturns were sorely surprised when their stock and bond holdings were losing value simultaneously at often the same rate in 2022. Cash is still paying next to nothing, at least not enough to keep up with inflation, and then we come to the stock or equity portion of your portfolio.

Stocks are touted as the best way to get a leg up on inflation, though stocks come with their own drawbacks.

Risk 2: Stock Market Volatility

Regardless of the current valuation of the market, there are always unknown and unforeseen risks to equities or stocks traded on public exchanges. You may have heard your broker or advisor say the stock market averages 6 to 10 percent per year, so why would you put your money anywhere else?

While there is some merit to these words of advice, you aren't getting the whole picture. Saying the stock market averages 6 to 10 percent per year is like me saying my wife and I run an average of thirty miles per week—but I only jog two of them. The reality is that the stock market doesn't make these returns in a linear fashion. This is what we call volatility (ups and downs/roller coaster rides).

The market goes through two types of periods: expansion and contraction, also known as bull and bear markets. Even though the long-term average has been very strong, the reality is that there are periods of time extending years—even decades—where you would have experienced little to no return.

These periods of bear markets and/or volatility can lead to losses not only in equities but also in the fixed-income portion of your portfolio. When the stock market as a whole is losing ground, such as during a recession, investments you thought of as consistent or reliable will

PURPOSE-BASED ASSET ALLOCATION

lose value, even those tried-and-true assets like bonds, blue chip stocks or dividend-paying stocks. This wasn't a problem during your working career, as you didn't need the money. If you were making periodic deposits to your investments out of your paycheck, you would purchase more quantities of asset classes that were depressed in value and less when they were overvalued, effectively allowing you to time the market without having to know anything about it. This is what is known as dollar-cost averaging, a fantastic strategy that all should employ while saving for retirement.[3]

The following chart shows what this dollar-cost averaging can look like. The column for Account #1 represents an account that purchases $1,000 of shares each month. If the stock value is up, the account purchases fewer. If stock values are down, the account purchases more. Compare that valuation with Account #2, where an initial $5,000 was used to purchase 250 shares.

DOLLAR-COST AVERAGING

	Account #1: $1,000 monthly contributions	VS		Account #2: a one-time $5,000 contribution (250 shares)
Month	Share Price	Shares Bought	Account #1 Value	Account #2 Value
January	$20	50	$ 1,000	$ 5,000
February	$16	63	$ 1,800	$ 4,000
March	$12	83	$ 2,350	$ 3,000
April	$17	59	$ 4,329	$ 4,250
May	$23	43	$ 6,857	$ 5,750

(This is a hypothetical example that is demonstrating a mathematical principle. It does not illustrate any investment products and does not show past or future performance of any specific investment.)

The opposite is true as your needs change in retirement from accumulation to deaccumulation. Retirees often say they are out of time when they get to retirement. Why? Because you are going to have immediate needs for a portion of your funds that you didn't have prior, which is called cash flow. As you begin taking distributions from your portfolio, the market will inevitably go down, or at least some of the assets in your portfolio, and if income is indiscriminately taken from these investments, you will be violating a key rule of investing: "Buy low and sell high."

This is what put many retirees back to work following the dot-com bust and the financial crisis of 2008. If you were working, these down markets presented the opportunity to purchase cheap assets and let them rebound, but in retirement, you faced quite the opposite.

These potential losses present one of the greatest risks at the front end of your retirement. You can afford losses during your retirement, but you cannot afford severe losses on the front end. In other words, you may experience a market that averages 8 percent per year, and if the good returns are at the front end and the bad are on the back, you're OK. If you flip those returns with the same average rate of return? You may run out of funds during retirement. Simply saying, "I only need to average 6 percent per year in retirement" and "I've done better in the past" doesn't work—this is what is called "sequence of returns risk." When interviewed on the *Retire With Purpose*™ podcast, Dr. Wade Pfau, professor of retirement income at the American College of Financial Services, had this to say about sequence of returns risk: "The stock market on average earns 7 percent after inflation, so 7 percent should be a safe withdrawal rate with 100 percent stock and, unfortunately, that's not how things work. The idea of sequence of returns risk and the amount you can spend in retirement might be less than what you

PURPOSE-BASED ASSET ALLOCATION

think based on the average market returns over that (your specific) retirement period."

The following are charts depicting different risks encountered by two retirees. Steve retired in 1990 and enjoyed appreciable gains following one down year at the beginning of retirement. Bill retired in 2000 and experienced three years of unfavorable returns at the beginning of retirement. Overall, the two men will likely face the same "average" return in retirement, but their account values will be very different depending on the order of their returns and whether losses occurred earlier or later in retirement.

End of Year	Market Return[1]	Withdrawal	IRA Account Balance
1990	-4.34%	$ 30,000	$ 449,602
1991	20.32%	$ 30,000	$ 504,865
1992	4.17%	$ 30,000	$ 494,667
1993	13.72%	$ 30,000	$ 528,419
1994	2.14%	$ 30,000	$ 509,085
1995	33.45%	$ 30,000	$ 639,340
1996	26.01%	$ 30,000	$ 767,829
1997	22.64%	$ 30,000	$ 904,873
1998	16.10%	$ 30,000	$ 1,015,728
1999	25.22%	$ 30,000	**$ 1,234,328**

Steve: Income and Seqence of Returns

JOB OPTIONAL

End of Year	Market Return[1]	Withdrawal	IRA Account Balance
2000	-6.18%	$ 30,000	$ 440,954
2001	-7.10%	$ 30,000	$ 381,776
2002	-16.76%	$ 30,000	$ 292,819
2003	25.32%	$ 30,000	$ 329,364
2004	3.15%	$ 30,000	$ 308,794
2005	-0.61%	$ 30,000	$ 277,094
2006	16.29%	$ 30,000	$ 287,345
2007	6.43%	$ 30,000	$ 273,892
2008	-33.84%	$ 30,000	$ 161,359
2009	18.82%	$ 30,000	**$ 156,081**

Bill: Income and Seqence of Returns

PURPOSE-BASED ASSET ALLOCATION

End of Year	Market Return[1]	Withdrawal	IRA Account Balance
1990	-4.34%	$ 30,000	$ 449,602
1991	20.32%	$ 30,000	$ 504,865
1992	4.17%	$ 30,000	$ 494,667
1993	13.72%	$ 30,000	$ 528,419
1994	2.14%	$ 30,000	$ 509,085
1995	33.45%	$ 30,000	$ 639,340
1996	26.01%	$ 30,000	$ 767,829
1997	22.64%	$ 30,000	$ 904,873
1998	16.10%	$ 30,000	$ 1,015,728
1999	25.22%	$ 30,000	**$ 1,234,328**

(These are hypothetical examples demonstrating a mathematical principle. They do not illustrate any investment products and do not show the past or future performance of any specific investment.)

Risk 3: Longevity and Health Care Costs

The longer you live, the higher the probability you will face market crashes or corrections and today, retirees are living longer than ever. This probably won't change, either. With advances in medical technology and our country's renewed focus on healthy eating and exercise, someone retiring at the age of sixty may spend more time in retirement than they did working. Prominent author, lecturer and founder of Edelman Financial Services, Ric Edelman, spoke on this topic, saying, "Your clients are going to live to 120, and, if you haven't built that into your financial plan, you're not running accurate projections for them."[4]

This means you will face a higher probability of not only running out of money in retirement but also higher potential health care costs and a rising cost of living. The longer you live, the more you are affected by inflation.

In addition, health care costs have historically seen much higher rates of inflation than other expenses you will face in retirement. You may think to yourself, "I am in great shape and take excellent care of myself, not to mention my genealogy," but those exact things may be what leads to higher health care costs as you live longer than those around you.

This is a risk often overlooked when planning for the retirement of a couple. On average, men have little chance of outliving their female counterparts, and if statistics become a reality, overlooking the continuation of retirement for a surviving spouse could be extremely detrimental.

Furthermore, I am afraid that, due to our aging population and nearly 10,000 people turning sixty-five every day, the costs of health care aren't going down anytime soon.[5]

PURPOSE-BASED ASSET ALLOCATION

A surviving spouse will see a loss of income, a greater impact of inflation, a higher probability of market volatility, increased taxes as a single-filer and a greater risk of long-term care expenses because they no longer have a spouse to rely on. These are just a few of the risks a surviving spouse will face that cannot be overlooked when structuring a solid retirement plan for two.

> "...80 percent of men die married, 80 percent of women die widowed... 70 percent to 80 percent of women will leave the financial advisor that they're working with right now if their husband dies within eighteen months, and the reason is the financial advisor is not working closely with them. The financial advisor's always been working with the husband."
>
> ~David Bach, *Smart Women Finish Rich: 9 Steps to Achieving Financial Security and Funding Your Dreams*

Likelihood of a 65-Year-Old Living to Age...

AGE	MALE SINGLE	FEMALE SINGLE	AT LEAST ONE MEMBER OF A COUPLE
85	45%	57%	76%
90	24%	35%	50%
95	8%	14%	21%[6]

Risk 4: Inflation Risks

The monetary stimulus from central banks globally has impacted our short-term inflation rates, indicating that we'll all continue to experience some inflation in the future. While it might not reach the heights observed in 2022 or those seen in the 1970s, the truth is that forecasting the precise short or long-term effects of inflation remains challenging. Thus, planning for it is as crucial as preparing for significant market downturns.

To better understand the impact of inflation, just ask yourself this question: what did you pay for your first home? Now, what did you pay for your last car? If you've been around long enough, you will find those numbers may be strikingly close together. That's inflation.

The longer your retirement, the higher the likelihood you will face some effects of inflation. Without adapting your strategy throughout retirement, you may be left with half of the purchasing power you had at the onset of retirement thirty years in—or worse.[7] This is where the L.I.F.E. planning pillar of Flexibility comes in.

Efficiency

Have you ever been to Mexico or the Caribbean and experienced one of those amphibious boat rides? My wife and I did. The attraction was called the "Amazing Amphibious Bus Tour." The Cayman Islands, located in the British West Indies, are known for clear blue water, powdery white sand beaches and great places for snorkeling. For our one-year anniversary, we decided to purchase tickets to ride on what looks like a large bus with gigantic windows that tours the city of George Town one minute and splashes into turquoise waters the next. It was a fun trip and an interesting ride, but there are tradeoffs to riding in a vehicle that does double duty as both a boat and a bus. As clever and entertaining

PURPOSE-BASED ASSET ALLOCATION

as our tour guide was, he could do little about the fact that the bus was slow. He could also not improve our comfort level. Even though the boat was labeled "unsinkable" because of the strategic insertion of foam in sections of the bus/boat's undercarriage, we were still afloat in a road vehicle that, despite all the reassurance given us by our driver/captain, seemed unseaworthy.

The amphibious bus (or hydra/terra, as some call it) reminds me of the financial strategies put in place by some financial advisors these days. Attempts to cobble together strategies that give you the best of both worlds often miss the mark completely.

Variable annuities are often touted as the silver bullet for retirees. They offer market participation for inflation protection, guaranteed income riders you cannot outlive and even death benefits for your loved ones after you're gone. The reality is that these elements come at a price, which often exceeds 4 percent per year. The end result is less growth for inflation protection than what is available in other market products, less guaranteed income than alternative guaranteed income products with a single focus and a taxable death benefit that comes at a higher cost than a tax-free life insurance policy.

> A VARIABLE ANNUITY IS A TYPE OF ANNUITY CONTRACT THAT ALLOWS FOR THE ACCUMULATION OF CAPITAL ON A TAX-DEFERRED BASIS. IT OFFERS INVESTORS THE OPPORTUNITY TO GENERATE HIGHER RATES OF RETURNS BY INVESTING IN EQUITY AND BOND SUBACCOUNTS.

I also commonly see retirees retire with a big "diversified" portfolio of stocks and bonds, or more likely mutual funds and exchange-traded funds, expecting this to cover all their retirement risks.[8]

If you're relying on this portfolio as your emergency fund, what happens if it's down 20 percent and an emergency strikes? How will you avoid selling when the market is down if you need to meet your monthly income requirements? How will it generate enough income to meet your health care expenses if you suddenly have a long-term care demand? These are just a few of the reasons you will need to use different tools to accomplish each of your specific goals. Otherwise, you are missing the full potential of covering each one. Clearly identify the purpose of each asset, and you will be well on your way to reaching your goal in a straight line of efficiency. Find the closest distance between two points.

> For more on this topic, check out the Podcast section of the Howard Bailey website and watch our video, "7 Principles to Help You Create Your Perfect Portfolio":
>
> HOWARDBAILEY.COM/263

Mind Off My Money, Money Off My Mind

The ultimate goal of structuring a solid financial plan for retirement is to have matters settled. I want you to answer this question for yourself: "What does retirement mean to me?"

I know at first it may seem like a silly question, but I have asked that question to literally thousands of retirees and pre-retirees, and the answers vary widely from freedom to time with family to pursuit of neglected interests. I have never had anyone answer "money." However, in every instance, I met these individuals and discussed specific concerns regarding money, whether at an event or in my office.

I hope to make this the last financial book you read during retirement so you can stop thinking about money and truly begin enjoying your retirement to the fullest.

For decades, you have probably been focused on accumulating money, and with the right plan, you can fulfill the true purpose of having the money in the first place, which is to deliver the freedom to pursue what is most meaningful to you in life.

This cannot be accomplished if your plan is dependent on constant best-case scenarios. Structuring a personalized Retire With Purpose™ Framework will not only allow you to identify a fulfilling purpose for retirement but will also allow you to live out that purpose without worrying about what's next in the stock market, politics or even your health. Of course, you may never be able to eliminate all your retirement concerns or risks. However, with a real plan, at least we can cover the risks that are most identifiable and play defense against the unknown. Then, you can decide what is most important to you.

TAKEAWAYS, ACTIONS AND NOTES

What are your biggest takeaways from this chapter?

_____

_____

_____

_____

_____

_____

_____

What are three action steps that you should work on now?

1. _____

2. _____

3. _____

What are three action steps for later?

1. _____

2. _____

3. _____

PURPOSE-BASED ASSET ALLOCATION

NOTES:

CHAPTER THREE
LIQUIDITY PLANNING

What if your adult child must move back in with you? What if your best friend wins an exotic trip, and you get an invite to tag along? What if you have a major unexpected repair to your car? What if the European trip you've dreamed of comes up at an unexpected discount but earlier than you budgeted for?

Whether it's an opportunity or something less fortunate, certain life happenings come at us quickly, and if you don't have liquidity— money in the bank, so to speak—you may be forced to forego opportunities or, worse, put them on a high-interest credit card.

Be Ready for the Unexpected

Studies have shown that it's not those who have more income, more investments or even more net worth who are the happiest and most financially secure.

Instead, those who are happiest possess the largest relative bank balances with cash readily available in the case of emergency. I have found this to be especially true for retirees due to the lessened financial flexibility provided by a fixed income.

You can no longer pick up a little extra overtime to fund those unexpected events. You're on your own. A rock-solid financial plan is your only option. Now, I am not suggesting you liquidate all investments and shift them into a bank account, but I am suggesting you ensure that you have an adequate emergency fund prior to stepping into retirement.

What that means to you may be different from the next person because any definitive amount is dependent on a couple of factors. At a minimum, we suggest you have at least six months' worth of your expenses put away in a bank account to be easily accessed in case the need arises. In some cases, we have liquidated investments or extended a retirement date to raise the funds—it's that important. Beyond that, the "right amount" is whatever helps you sleep at night, but only if it doesn't jeopardize your overall financial plan.

I have some clients who will set aside one to two years' worth of expenses to feel secure. In that case, you may want to look at alternatives to traditional banking products such as savings accounts, money markets or certificates of deposit. A conservative investment portfolio may make sense for a portion of these funds or even a properly structured insurance product.

I myself keep the funds needed to pay off our home mortgage in an overfunded cash-value life insurance policy. I maintain my mortgage interest deduction and defer my annual gains inside of my life insurance policy, which, if never needed, will pass on tax-free to my heirs via an enhanced death benefit. I can also use the death benefit while I am living

LIQUIDITY PLANNING

through an accelerated death benefit rider, providing some protection in the case of my disability or long-term care need.

In addition, I am averaging a higher net rate of return than what I pay on my mortgage balance. It's important to note that for this to work, you need to have the policy structured in such a way as to ensure you can't lose your original investment and that there are no penalties for early withdrawal.

I once had a client with an old life insurance policy they had funded for more than twenty years (getting them well past any surrender charges), from which they were netting annual returns of 4 percent per year, which, at the time, was substantially better than they could get at the bank. They moved funds from their bank account into the life insurance policy, dramatically increasing the annual returns on what they viewed as their emergency fund and increasing their death benefits as well. This particular policy had "living benefit" provisions allowing them to access the death benefit while living for things like a serious health crisis. Remember, if they never leverage the death benefit for "living benefits," then the value will pass tax-free to their heirs.

If you don't have a life insurance policy that has passed the surrender charge period, you may want to establish what is known as a modified endowment contract (MEC), essentially overfunding a life insurance policy and waiving the surrender charges to ensure the protection of the cash value, growth and liquidity in the case of emergency. If a policy becomes a MEC, it will be treated as a non-qualified annuity for tax purposes.

This is another example of maximizing the efficiency of your hard-earned life savings. The bottom line: Have an emergency fund, regardless of the size, so you know you can cover those unknown events during retirement.

JOB OPTIONAL

TAKEAWAYS, ACTIONS AND NOTES

What are your biggest takeaways from this chapter?

_____
_____
_____
_____
_____
_____
_____

What are three action steps that you should work on now?

1. _____
2. _____
3. _____

What are three action steps for later?

1. _____
2. _____
3. _____

LIQUIDITY PLANNING

NOTES:

CHAPTER FOUR

INCOME PLANNING

Without income, there cannot be retirement. There may not be a more important part of your retirement strategy than a comprehensive income plan that addresses longevity, market and tax risks. Simply setting a goal for a certain rate of return and regular distributions is not a retirement income strategy. Neither is generating enough dividends and interest to live off without touching the principal. Let me explain why it's much more than that.

> **A RATE OF RETURN (ROR) IS THE NET GAIN OR LOSS ON AN INVESTMENT OVER A SPECIFIED TIME PERIOD, EXPRESSED AS A PERCENTAGE OF THE INVESTMENT'S INITIAL COST.**

The 4 Percent Withdrawal Rule / Systematic Withdrawal Approach

Also known as the Prudent Man's Rule, the 4 Percent Withdrawal Rule was pioneered by a California-based financial advisor named William Bengen in 1994. It was then popularized by "the Trinity Study" in 1998 and later titled SAFEMAX for the maximum "safe" historical withdrawal rate. The idea is that retirees investing in a portfolio split between stocks and bonds could withdraw 4 percent from that portfolio in the first year of retirement. Then, the retirees could make inflation-adjusted withdrawals in subsequent years over a thirty-year retirement and most likely not deplete their savings (the key there being "most likely"). Bengen used historical data dating back to 1926. However, some things have changed, and many experts are questioning whether this rule still stands, given the ever-evolving economic environment.[9]

Without diving too deep into statistics, the bottom line is that a retiree doesn't get a significant amount of confidence regarding their retirement when there is any chance of total failure. Even if we can illustrate a 95 percent chance of success, that 5 percent chance of failure could happen tomorrow if you retire at the peak of a market, before a major stock market correction or even crash. In the end, using any set of purely market-based investments with an accompanying scheduled withdrawal rate is not a plan for the worst but, rather, a plan that is hoping for the best and planning for the best. Instead, you should be planning for the best and preparing for the worst.

Interest-Only Income Strategy

Another popular strategy relies on generating enough dividends or interest to cover any monthly retirement income needs. Similar to the concept of a 4 percent withdrawal, this strategy depends largely on

INCOME PLANNING

markets consistently performing well. Yet, the most glaring problem here is that most retirees haven't saved enough to live adequately off the interest income from their investments. The median retirement savings balance for those aged fifty-five through sixty-four is $185,000.[10] Even if you could generate a 6 percent return for annual income, you would only create $1,000 per month in pre-tax income, whereas the average American aged sixty-five and older spends $4,073 on a monthly basis.[11]

In many instances, when a client pushes their advisor to achieve these rates of yield on their investments, they end up taking on excessive degrees of risk using high-yield (also known as junk) bonds, long-term bonds, oil and gas partnerships, real estate investment trusts or even unstable high-yielding stocks. Even so, the highest quality large cap stocks may cut or even eliminate their dividends in a down market, and your bonds may default altogether. This is just another buy-and-hope approach, lending an equal degree of uncertainty to your retirement as the 4 Percent Withdrawal Rule.

Real Income Strategies

There is no one-size-fits-all approach when it comes to implementing an income strategy for your retirement years. Some annuity pushers may tell you to guarantee all your lifetime income in retirement, while your securities broker might say you need to live off municipal bonds or dividend income.

The reality is that you must decide after you are presented with all the options. Each option has its own pros and cons. Since we've already mentioned guaranteed lifetime income, which may sound overwhelmingly appealing, why don't we start there?

Guaranteed Lifetime Income

The word "guarantee" can strike fear into the hearts of a retiree, just as much as the word "annuity."

There is valid reason to be concerned, too. In recent decades, we have seen a proliferation of financial scams and Ponzi schemes typically carrying such a word in their marketing pitches.

If you are being promised outlandish returns without the risk of principal losses, then yes, be afraid. Be very afraid.

However, if this word is being used in relation to the insurance world instead of the investment world, there may be validity to these guarantees. The downside will most likely be the lack of long-term growth and flexibility in contrast to the world of investments. In return, you will receive guarantees that a stockbroker will never be able to match, which may be worth some tradeoffs; it's up to you.

How Safe Is That "Guarantee," Really?

There is little opportunity for true guarantees in this world. As the saying goes, "The only things in life that are guaranteed are death and taxes." Annuity guarantees, however, are about as close as they get in the world of finance.[12] Understanding how insurance companies are allowed to even use this word comes down to something known as the "legal reserve system."

The legal reserve system requires by law that certain levels of funds be set aside and maintained at all times to cover future obligations of the issuing company. The Federal Deposit Insurance Corporation (FDIC) is one example of a legal reserve system for banks, requiring them to have certain minimum guaranteed reserves available to satisfy their

INCOME PLANNING

financial obligations. Some legal reserve systems require 100 percent reserves (dollar-for-dollar) to be kept in place. Other systems may require only a few pennies on each dollar of obligations. Certificates of deposit, for instance, are backed by the legal federal reserves maintained by the FDIC. While the FDIC backs deposits up to $250,000 per Social Security number per institution, banks aren't required to keep 100 percent dollar-for-dollar legal reserves on hand to back up these deposits.[13] Investments, such as stocks and bonds, don't carry reserve requirements, and that's one reason you may have seen some stocks and corporate bonds become completely worthless throughout history.

Savings vehicles backed by a legal reserve system include banks, government bonds and insurance companies. We've discussed banks and understand that the Federal Reserve can print its own money to back up government bonds, but how does an insurance company's legal reserve system operate?

The easiest way to describe this is to compare the way they operate with the way the banking system works. Banks are typically required by the Board of Governors of the Federal Reserve System (FRB) to keep a fraction of a dollar on hand for every dollar they lend.[14] In March 2020, the Board actually reduced the reserve requirement ratios to zero in response to the COVID-19 pandemic.[15] We cannot say banks are not safe, as they are still backed by the FDIC, and the government is able to hit the printing presses quickly to fill this gap.

I'm not saying banks aren't a secure place to put your money, but it's interesting to compare banks with insurance companies and see which ones are on the most solid footing when it comes to required reserves.

The states, rather than the federal government, regulate insurance companies. What significance does that have? Insurance companies are required by law to follow the guidelines of up to fifty states versus

63

one federal entity—if they intend to operate nationally, that is.[16] "If insurance companies aim to operate nationally in the U.S., they must navigate and comply with the regulatory frameworks of potentially all fifty states, as opposed to a single federal entity." This state-by-state approach, as outlined by the National Association of Insurance Commissioners (NAIC), results in a complex regulatory landscape. Unlike banks, insurance companies must have dollar-for-dollar in reserves. In addition, while banks are allowed to invest their working capital in a wide range of investments, from mortgages to business loans, insurance companies are required to keep the majority of their customer's funds in relatively more conservative investments, such as U.S. government bonds and highly-rated corporate bonds. If they make more speculative investments, they must use their own capital, not the portion that is required by law to be set aside to settle potential customer claims.

The National Organization of Life and Health Insurance (NOLHGA) has stated that the fixed insurance industry is now better prepared than other areas of the financial industry to withstand national economic challenges and that in the eighteen months leading up to June 2009, not a single life insurer had to be liquidated as a result of the economic downturn. Furthermore, there has not been a single failure of a fixed insurance carrier of national significance since 1994. This sharply contrasts with the twenty-five banks that failed in 2008, followed by almost 400 banks that met the same fate over the next three years.[17]

Beyond its primary reserves, an insurance company further reduces risk through the use and requirement of surplus capital. Throughout my professional career, I've found that most insurance companies hold somewhere between 5 percent and 15 percent in excess reserves. I've even seen companies in excess of 50 percent, or $150, on hand for every $100 they owe. When the surplus capital drops below the minimum

INCOME PLANNING

required by the state in which the company is located, the state may put the insurance company into receivership and take over. This is rare, but it has happened. When it does, the state takes over the legal responsibility to make sure client funds are transferred to a stronger insurance company as soon as possible. Client accounts of an insurance company are highly valuable, which is why (in most cases) a stronger insurance company is very willing to pay money and acquire those assets. What happens in the rare case where no buyer can be found to take over those assets and liabilities? This is when reinsurers step into the picture.

Reinsurance is the process by which part or all of the insurer's risk is assumed by other insurance companies in return for part of the premium paid by the insurer. Many primary insurers have purchased reinsurance from as many as ten different companies. Despite all these safety nets being in place, it is still prudent to carry out your due diligence when placing your assets with an insurance company. Focus on the assets and investments of the insurance company before depositing your hard-earned dollars with them.

I have never heard a retiree say they hate their pension. The reality is that their pension is just another form of an annuity. An annuity is an investment vehicle utilized by insurance companies to provide investment options, including a potential income stream. There are many different types of annuities that may offer guaranteed income options. Previously, the responsibility for retirees' pensions—and the associated funding liability—fell on the employer.

> **I HAVE NEVER HEARD A RETIREE SAY THEY HATE THEIR PENSION.**

Since the introduction of defined-contribution plans, such as 401(k)s, today's truth is that you must create your own version of the pension yesterday's retirees enjoyed.

This is one of the biggest hurdles of today's retirement: You have focused on the growth and return on your money for decades, and you must now shift that focus to income and the return of your money. There will be trade-offs when it comes to flexibility and the long-term return of your assets regarding annuities. However, I have found over the years that many retirees are not as concerned with what they might leave behind as they are with having certainty about their returns.

> "More dangerous yet is the shift in focus away from retirement income to return on investment that has come with the introduction of saver-managed DC plans: Investment decisions are now focused on the value of the funds, the returns on investment they deliver, and how volatile those returns are. Yet the primary concern of the saver remains what it always has been: 'Will I have sufficient income in retirement to live comfortably?'"
>
> ~*Harvard Business Review,* "The Crisis in Retirement Planning"[18]

A common challenge is that many individuals mistakenly group all annuities under the label of "immediate annuities." In reality, immediate annuities represent just a small subset of a broader range of annuity products. A common challenge is that many individuals mistakenly group all annuities under the label of "immediate annuities." In reality, immediate annuities represent just a small subset of a broader range of annuity products.

Immediate Annuity

An **immediate annuity**, also known as a single premium immediate annuity (SPIA), is a vehicle in which you make a lump sum deposit. As a result, you receive an income stream that could be structured to provide income over a specified period or even a lifetime or two. This is a double-edged sword. You have a total loss of control over the lump sum, and the insurance company keeps whatever funds are left in the contract in the event of your early death. BUT—if the annuity covers you (or even you and your spouse) for a lifetime, you may outlive the amount of money you used to fund the contract, and the insurance company will continue your payments.

> An immediate annuity, also known as an income or single premium immediate annuity (spia), is a contract between you and an insurance company designed for income purposes only. Unlike a deferred annuity, an immediate annuity skips the accumulation stage and begins paying out income either immediately or within a year after you have purchased it with a single, lump-sum payment. Spias are also called immediate payment annuities, income annuities, lifetime annuities and immediate annuities.

In a low-interest rate environment or a period of high inflation, you may, of course, be locked into an income that is disadvantageous. These vehicles may come in handy, though, if you have the goal of creating a period of guaranteed income of, say, five or ten years. This is especially the case with nonqualified or after-tax funds, as the annuitization feature will allow you to spread out your taxable gain equally over the term of the contract. In addition, if you select a set period and pass away during the distribution period, the payments typically continue on to your heirs.

This is something my dad took advantage of with some of the nonqualified annuities he purchased over the years. He previously had fixed annuities, which he later transferred into fixed index annuities and then annuitized years later to spread out the taxable gain that was deferred over the time he held those investments.

> A fixed annuity is a type of annuity contract that allows for the accumulation of capital on a tax-deferred basis. In exchange for a lump sum of capital, a life insurance company credits the annuity account with a guaranteed fixed interest rate while guaranteeing the principal investment. A fixed annuity can be annuitized to provide the annuitant with a guaranteed income payout for a specified term or for life.

Utilizing a SPIA in such a way can buy you time to allow your at-risk investments to endure the continuing volatility of the stock market with much higher return potential.

Fixed Annuities

The next most basic form of an annuity is by far the easiest to understand—operating much like the familiar CD but backed by an insurance company instead of the FDIC or banking institution selling the product. A fixed annuity offers a fixed rate of return over a fixed period. Typically, the return is significantly higher than what would be offered through a bank product but accompanied by stiffer penalties for early withdrawal. Terms of surrender charge periods can vary over two- to ten-year periods, over which time you typically have some sort of penalty-free withdrawal in the amount of interest earned (or 5 to 10 percent of the account value).

These products can make for a good alternative to an ultra-conservative CD or even a more secure alternative to the investment-grade bond market. Over the years, I have had many clients who found these products to be a good fit for a large portion of their retirement savings.

MEET BOB AND CHARLENE

Bob and Charlene came to my office after they encountered a significant level of frustration with their investments over the previous couple of years. They were strangers to the investment world. Their wealth was mostly made up of farmland that had been passed down for generations. Bob and Charlene had an interesting situation when they found their children were not interested in continuing the family legacy as farmers into the future. They decided to sell the farm. In addition, like many farmers—including those in my own family—this couple had very limited experiences outside of the farm. For those of you who don't know, the demands of farming can be intense. Families on small farms wake up at the crack of dawn and often manage to get more done in the hours before the sun comes up than the average American can do in a day.

After Bob and Charlene sold their farm, they found a local investment broker who promised them higher returns than they had ever seen in the farming business. The proposal involved a blend of stock market and high-risk, limited-partnership-type investments. Two years after the initial sale of approximately half of their farmland, Bob and Charlene had seen ups and downs that left them with about 10 percent less in value than they started with—and this was during a strong bull market. They told me they never wanted to see their accounts go down in value again. They just couldn't take the stress.

Bob and Charlene had never experienced the roller coaster runs of the market before, in contrast to the average 401(k) investors who experience multiple recessions over their lifetimes (and they may not have needed the risk, either). They were much like my father after he sold his apartments; he couldn't stomach losses on wealth that had taken so much energy to create.

Bob and Charlene could not handle traditional market-based investments but were ecstatic about a modest fixed rate that was guaranteed to credit interest to their account on a monthly basis without ever having to see the account dip in value.

The interest generated from their new fixed annuities more than covered their monthly expenses and allowed them to travel, experiencing things they could never have done had they held onto the farm. Furthermore, they may never have had the confidence to spend their money while it was fluctuating up and down in the stock market. Bob and Charlene continued to sell more of the farm and more farming equipment while opening more fixed annuities that offered the certainty they wanted for their retirement years.

This wouldn't be the right fit for everyone, but it was the right fit for them, offering exactly the tool they were looking for in their retirement. Other individuals and retirees, on the other hand, are willing to accept a little volatility or lack of predictability with more upside potential than others.

Fixed Index Annuities

That leads us to our next major type of annuity, the **fixed index annuity**, which has grown dramatically in popularity over the last couple of decades.[19] The fixed index annuity offers the principal guarantees of a fixed annuity with more upside potential closer to that offered in a traditional stock market investment. Returns are typically tied to some type of stock market index, such as the S&P 500, SPDR Gold Trust or even actively managed indices, after which limits are put on annual returns.[20] Returns can be limited in many ways through such factors as participation rates, caps or spreads.

- A *participation rate* will offer a percentage of returns in whatever index it is tracking, such as 75 percent of the returns in the S&P 500 without downside risk.
- *Cap rates* limit returns to a specified percentage, such as 10 percent of the returns in the S&P 500, without downside risk.
- With *spreads*, also known as hurdles, your returns must exceed a certain percentage before you receive credits to your account, such as 2 percent per year, after which excess returns are credited to the client's account.

INDEXED ANNUITIES ARE INSURANCE CONTRACTS THAT, DEPENDING ON THE CONTRACT, MAY OFFER A GUARANTEED ANNUAL INTEREST RATE AND SOME PARTICIPATION IN A STOCK MARKET INDEX.

Arguably, the most attractive aspect of a fixed index annuity is the periodic crediting—after which your contract locks in the increase in value of the account.

This can occur annually or maybe even as far out as every five years. On the other hand, any growth accrued over that period leading up to the lock-in date is earned and cannot be lost to downward market movements over the following lock-in term.

The primary downside of fixed index annuities is the same as the fixed annuity—you will be forced to take on some type of term with limited liquidity provisions. This could mean having a withdrawal limit of up to 5 to 10 percent of the account value per year or a contract term limit of five to twenty years.

The following chart illustrates how the "lock-in" provision of an FIA allows it to measure up against a stock market product, both in the short run or over a longer time period.

The index drops, but your contract value holds steady.

Following a year of negative index performance, the market heads up. The index does not have to make up previous losses before your annuity can earn additional interest. Your accumulation value can increase in any year in which a positive index change takes place, thanks to an annual reset.[21]

Obviously, the more flexibility you are willing or able to give up, the more potential for interest credits you will be offered in return. Stockbrokers most often cite the limited returns and flexibility these vehicles offer as the reason people shouldn't use them.

Over time, I found that many retirees often aren't looking for stock-market-like returns anymore. Instead, they are seeking modest returns without the concern of losing half of their life savings in the market or facing obstacles such as bond defaults during retirement. My dad is one of those people, often saying he has saved enough for retirement and that he just needs to make 4 to 6 percent and not lose it. Most of his life savings are in various indexed products, from annuities to life insurance, offering him the principal protection he seeks and the growth potential that enables him to be content. Some of the people we have worked with over the years still want the guaranteed income offered through such things as SPIAs but want to maintain more flexibility and growth potential as well.

Fixed Index Annuities with a GLWB Rider

Some fixed index annuities may offer something called a **guaranteed lifetime withdrawal** benefit rider (GLWB).[22] You might think of riders as sidecars to the main event—you have all the principal protection and growth potential of a fixed index annuity, but the "sidecar" rider also puts income guarantees on top of your basic policy.

To understand this concept, think about it as a T-chart. On one side is what we call your "accumulation value," acting like the fixed index annuity we discussed earlier. I prefer to think of this side of the chart as your "real money." These are the funds you can walk away with after the surrender charge period or which you can leave to your beneficiaries as a lump-sum death benefit.

> **A guaranteed lifetime withdrawal benefit (glwb) is a rider to an annuity contract that allows for lifetime guaranteed withdrawals to be made from an annuity during the owner's lifetime without penalty. The owner typically pays for the glwb with an extra percentage of fees based on the total value of the annuity contract.**

The other side of the T-chart represents the value of a potential future income stream known as a Guaranteed Lifetime Withdrawal Benefit. The value of your GLWB rider can grow in various ways but will usually carry some type of enhanced growth benefit over what is offered on the accumulation value ("real money") side. It may come in the form of a guaranteed annual return rate, a multiple of interest credited to the accumulation value or a lock-in rate that occurs more regularly—as frequently as daily.

This rider side of your T-chart is a calculation of the amount of income your contract will guarantee for the rest of your life—typically expressed as a percentage dependent on the age of the owner or beneficiary of the account. The insurance company will use this to calculate the income checks they send to you, but should you choose to take your money out of the contract at the end of your surrender period, this is not the side of the T-chart that you can walk away with. Think about the potential of outliving your life savings. You insure your car and home, so why not insure the biggest risk you face in retirement?

INCOME PLANNING

Accumulation Value "Real $"	GLWB Value "Income $"

My mom had an annuity like this of her own, purchased just prior to the financial collapse of 2008. She deposited her IRA value into an account where she was offered approximately 60 percent of the gains in the market, locked in every two years (the left side of the T-chart). In addition, she added a GLWB rider, guaranteeing her an 8 percent annual rate of return on funds to be used for future retirement income (the right side of the T-chart).

As a result, not only did she never experience the 2008 losses to her principal, but her GLWB value grew at 8 percent, compounded annually for future retirement income needs. At the age of sixty-five, she was guaranteed an annual withdrawal of 5.5 percent of the GLWB value per year for the rest of her life. As a teacher with a meager pension and spousal Social Security benefits, this offered her the ability to fill the gap in her expenses on a guaranteed basis without being concerned by the market volatility she may experience in her other investments.

Whatever she didn't spend would be left behind to me. Furthermore, since she funded it by rolling over some of her IRA, she didn't mind losing out on some flexibility—because of the tax implications of her traditional IRA, she was never going to take a large distribution from these funds and wasn't looking to them for liquidity.

MEET ROBERT AND CHERYL

I came across a couple, Robert and Cheryl, who were looking to purchase an immediate annuity to have a source of guaranteed income during their retirement years. They weren't sure when they would need to begin taking income during retirement. They were still enjoying their careers and didn't know exactly when they would retire.

Rather than stuffing them into an immediate annuity contract, which would immediately begin generating income they didn't yet need, we used a fixed index annuity with a GLWB rider, giving them more control over the future of their contract.

In addition, for each year that Robert and Cheryl deferred taking income from the annuity, their guaranteed income payouts increased. For some who are unsure of an exact retirement date but are looking for something to fall back on if they decide to quit working tomorrow, fixed index annuities with income riders can be a solid option.

Robert and Cheryl said it changed the way they lived and worked. They realized they weren't at the mercy of the market, and regardless of when they decided they were fed up with working, they knew they would be able to retire. This gave them the ability to enter "Job Optional" status, knowing they could retire at any time. Still, for some, even the upside potential offered in a fixed index annuity— with rider options—just isn't enough.

Variable Annuities

Variable annuities have declined in popularity due to a high degree of negative publicity attributable to excessive fees found therein.[23] As I mentioned previously in my narrative on efficiency, variable annuities have often been peddled as a so-called silver bullet for retirement. Financial professionals sell these products because of their upside potential and auxiliary guarantees, but it's important to remember that they all come at a serious cost. When making a deposit into a variable annuity, the first thing to understand is you are purchasing a "security." Far from the usual associations with the word "security," when we talk about security products in finance, we're talking about products that can lose value. Fixed and fixed index annuities are not classified as securities because you cannot lose your original principal due to market fluctuations.

Variable annuities essentially invest your money in mutual funds or exchange-traded funds until you begin taking income. At the time you turn on income, your income is calculated based on the performance of the mutual funds or exchange-traded funds that underlie your investment. This gives you more upside potential but also means you could lose money and suffer through retirement with an income based on an asset that took heavy losses in a market correction.

One attractive part of a variable annuity is the tax-deferral feature inherently found within all types of annuities. This allows your capital gains, dividends and interest to be deferred until the withdrawal of the funds in the future, much like a non-deductible IRA. It may only benefit the wealthiest of Americans in the highest of tax brackets, though. The downside of annuities is your distributions are always taxed as ordinary income rather than the more preferential capital gains or dividend rates. This is where you must weigh the cost of variable annuities heavily.

These products not only contain the costs and ongoing fees associated with the mutual funds or exchange-traded funds in which your money is invested, but you also must pay a separate charge for the insurance product wrapper itself, most commonly known as a mortality and expense charge. These charges vary widely and are typically more than 1 percent per year. However, they can be significantly less.

> A non-deductible ira is in many ways the same as a traditional ira. The contribution limits are the same, the money grows tax-deferred and to be eligible to contribute, you must have received earned income.
>
> The difference is, with a nondeductible ira, you aren't allowed to deduct your contribution from your income taxes like you can with a traditional ira.

I once had a high-income earning client in the highest marginal tax bracket with a substantial portion of his wealth in after-tax accounts generating significant taxable gains, which dramatically reduced his annual returns. We found a low-cost variable annuity offering low-cost exchange-traded funds as investment options; the monthly costs of the account were only twenty dollars per month. After projecting after-tax returns of traditional investments outside of the variable annuity in contrast to those within a variable annuity, it was more advantageous to pay the low cost for the tax-deferred wrapper.

I convey this to demonstrate I don't definitively dislike variable annuities—each product can have its place at the table. (And it's important for you to keep an open mind and set aside your bias before beginning your retirement planning.) Unfortunately, this is not the way most variable annuities are sold or used. In my experience, this is one investment that is typically misunderstood by those who aren't well acquainted with financial services.

Variable annuities have their place, but for many, they are one of the worst investments you could make with your retirement savings—so exercise caution.

ANNUITY QUICK-LOOK

IMMEDIATE	FIXED	FIXED INDEX	FIXED INDEX WITH GLWB	VARIABLE
Guaranteed income for a set period or lifetime	Fixed rate of return for a set period	Principal protection with returns tied to a specified market-based index	Same as Fixed Index with added feature of guaranteed lifetime income	Market risk to principal with ability to add various riders for income or death benefit guarantees

When it comes to creating a guaranteed lifetime income strategy, you may want to evaluate various SPIA and GLWB options. This will be the only way to truly guarantee that you will never run out of income during retirement, regardless of market fluctuations. Any product comes at a cost, of course; with fixed and fixed index annuities, you can easily see you will be giving up the growth potential and flexibility that traditional market-based investment options offer. I tend to lean away from having too high a concentration of annuities, opting instead to do my income planning through strategies we will soon discuss, such as flooring, segmented income or flexible withdrawal strategies. However, I am often surprised by how many retirees are willing to concede upside potential and flexibility in exchange for greater certainty in retirement, exemplifying the uniqueness we all have when it comes to structuring the appropriate retirement income strategy.

MEET TERRY

Terry was retiring from BF Goodrich after years of working on the factory floor. When our vice president, Marshal Johnson, and I first walked into our conference room and began reviewing Terry's current investments, his situation seemed pretty straightforward. Everything was saved in his 401(k) plan from work, with very little after-tax savings available. Terry said he hadn't looked at his statements in years; he just plugged away, pouring monthly contributions into his plan along with a generous employer match.

He said the day before he came to visit us was the first time he had looked at his statements in years—he was dumbfounded to realize he was a millionaire. There was a little over $1 million in his retirement plan from work, and he wanted to retire in a few short years at the age of sixty-two.

After reviewing various retirement income strategies, we found Terry could potentially double or triple the value of his accounts over his lifetime by using more of a market-based strategy with greater risk and still satisfy his retirement income needs. On the other side of the spectrum, we could use a strategy that focused on preserving his principal and guaranteeing him a lifetime of income.

Terry told us his heirs would be blown away if their dad even left behind a couple hundred thousand dollars, let alone $1 million or more. He went on to share with us that he never wanted to think about the stock market and didn't want to depend on the market doing average to even succeed. He never wanted to worry about the Dow dropping several hundred points in a day. He focused on the guaranteed options offered by annuity products because his main concern was knowing he would have enough income to last the rest of his life.

The last time Terry came in to visit with us, he mentioned his children wanted to know what we discussed. Terry went on to share that his children have always known him as a bit of a tightwad, but now, when there's something he wants to do, he does it! He no longer frets about the market or if he has enough. Instead, he spends his time focused on what he enjoys. Terry spends his time with grandkids and tinkering with old cars. He even purchased an old Firebird he had his eye on for years, just like when he was a kid. Terry was able to spend with confidence because he had a Retire With Purpose™ Framework built just for him.

Many individuals we work with aren't willing to give up as much flexibility as Terry was and are often seeking to leave behind as much as possible in the way of a legacy for the next generation. In that respect, you may want to evaluate some of the following alternatives for your very own retirement income strategy.

Flooring

Flooring is a variation of a traditional guaranteed lifetime income strategy that offers more flexibility and upside potential, simply with fewer guarantees. To begin the planning process with this strategy, you will need to identify and separate your paychecks from your "play checks" during retirement. In other words, what expenses will you have during retirement that you simply cannot live without, and which would you be able to give up, either periodically or all together in a worst-case scenario?

At the start of retirement, you might realize that spending three months a year in a warmer climate or the yearly vacation you intend to take with your grandkids is not a need. But, when push comes to shove, you spent your whole life saving to be able to do these things, and you're going to do them whether it puts your retirement income strategy in jeopardy or not.

There are those, however, who have enough inherent financial discipline to follow a flooring strategy, guaranteeing the income they cannot live without and utilizing at-risk income strategies to supplement your "play checks," such as systematic withdrawal, interest, dividend, bond laddering strategies or even a blend.

During my interview with Dr. Wade Pfau on the *Retire With Purpose*™ podcast, he had this to say regarding using annuities as a flooring strategy: "If you have a certain amount of expenses per year, say $80,000 or whatever the case may be, we'll first look at things like Social Security, which is a guaranteed lifetime income, if you have any other pension, that sort of thing. And then, if there's still a gap, rather than trying to manage your whole retirement through these distributions from an investment portfolio, look at using income guarantees, an annuity offering lifetime income protection. This can help manage the longevity risk of not knowing how long you're going to live and help manage that sequence of returns risk, where having to take distributions from a declining portfolio balance becomes increasingly risky in retirement. Basing that more on insurance as the first building block can be a more prudent approach."[24]

MEET BILL AND BROOKE

Bill and Brooke fit the bill perfectly. With substantial pre-tax and after-tax savings (more than enough to handle their retirement income needs), they decided to structure a guaranteed lifetime income strategy with their pre-tax retirement savings. Then, they structured a portion of their after-tax savings to generate dividend income from equities. The income they expected from the equities was income they didn't think they necessarily needed—they had Social Security, pensions and their annuities, after all—but Bill and Brooke wanted the flexibility to know they could get a couple thousand extra dollars a month if they decided to live an extravagant year from time to time or gift more money to their children.

For them, flooring provided the security they needed and the flexibility they desired. Most recently, they wanted to take their grandkids on a Disney cruise: all nine grandkids plus their eight parents! The flexibility this plan offered was perfect for their lifestyle, and the flooring gave them the confidence they needed to do those little extra things every so often. For others desiring more growth potential and flexibility than a flooring strategy offers, it may be worth evaluating a segmented income strategy with varying degrees of risk.

Segmented Income

One of my personal favorite income strategies is a segmented income strategy, which provides for significant upside over the years while offering the psychological protection most retirees need to succeed. Retirement income strategies often fail because retirees panic during a down market. Why? Because everything was stuffed into an investment portfolio without specifically identifying which pieces of the portfolio would be spent down first. As a result, when the market tanks, retirees liquidate investments without discrimination and may never recover.

A segmented income strategy addresses the problem of immediate market volatility and gives a sort of buffer to buy themselves time to continue to invest funds needed to replace their first leg of income at some point in the future (typically five to ten years).

Once we have identified the income someone needs from the investment portfolio, we begin by segmenting off portions of the portfolio to be spent at different stages over the course of retirement. These are usually split into two to four different segments, depending on the amount of time a person expects to spend in retirement. The segments include a variety of investments or insurance products offering varying degrees of security and potential.

The first leg of income needs will be structured to satisfy five to ten years' worth of retirement income needs, dependent on available products and the client's desire for income security. This first leg of income could be generated using an annuity, conservative investment portfolio or bond ladder—it's important that the first leg of income be conservatively allocated, if not guaranteed.

Essentially, we are creating an anti-anxiety pill for retirement to allow your other investments to endure the market's ups and downs just as you did during your working years without causing panic. I have heard many retirees over the years say they need to get out of the market because they can't take the risk anymore. "Why?" I ask. They always say it's because they don't have the time they previously had to make up the losses.

What they aren't realizing is they still have a significant investment life left that may last another twenty to thirty years or more. The difference is that you now have monthly income needs you didn't have during your working years. Segmented income strategies can be helpful because they can buy you time to continue investing the funds you don't immediately need in more aggressive investments or allocations for long-term growth. This allows our second and third legs of income needs to take on greater risk and potential for growth. If a major market downturn occurs, you know your immediate income needs are taken care of for a period on the funds that either suffered no or minor losses.

INCOME PLANNING

The second and third legs of income have suffered losses to increasing degrees but have time to recover.

Your second leg of income assets may be structured in a more moderate allocation to be used five to ten years down the road, while your third leg may be structured in a more aggressive allocation fifteen to twenty years down the road or more. I like to say we are making you young again.

MEET RORY AND TINA

I once worked with a couple, Rory and Tina, who leaned toward the segmented strategy for their retirement years. When they retired at sixty-two and filed for early Social Security income, they had a gap to fill since they didn't have a pension benefit from their employer.

We used an annuity guaranteed to satisfy the first ten years of their retirement income needs. Then, we set aside additional funds to be invested in a moderate-risk investment portfolio of exchange-traded funds and individual stocks to be left alone to grow for the next ten years. After that, Rory and Tina would use those funds to satisfy their income needs for the following ten years.

As a result, we had satisfied twenty years of retirement income needs, taking them into their early eighties. Due to potential longevity, Rory and Tina wanted to plan on needing income into their early to mid-nineties, so we established a third leg of income in a more aggressive investment portfolio to be left alone for the next twenty years or more.

If you think about it, Rory and Tina were investing as if they were sixty-two on their first leg of income needs, fifty-two on their second leg of income needs and forty-two on their third leg of income needs. They were now able to wrap their heads around taking risk with their retirement funds, knowing the funds they don't need for a decade could dip 10 or 20 percent in a major market downturn, and the funds they won't need for twenty years may lose 20 or 30 percent, but also that they had bought themselves the time to make up the losses.

A strategy such as this is not meant to be static. Over time, we will need to rebalance the accounts as we spend down the first leg of income and experience growth in the second and third legs. The funds from our more aggressive investments will need to be shifted to a more conservative position to be more protective of our gains over time. Another interesting strategy is known as a flexible withdrawal strategy, which we will cover next.

Flexible Withdrawal Strategy

A **flexible withdrawal strategy** is just that: it's flexible! It may require a more hands-on approach than some of the more set-it-and-forget-it strategies discussed previously. Nevertheless, it might also offer

INCOME PLANNING

significantly more growth potential as well.

Within a flexible withdrawal strategy, we will structure a portfolio with a variety of different investments offering enough diversification for us to know there will always be a place for us to go—even in a down market—to generate income without violating the cardinal rule of investments ("buy low and sell high"). One of the biggest risks for retirees is the chance they may suffer a significant loss and be forced to sell depressed assets in a poor market, but a flexible withdrawal strategy can address this by holding a significant number of uncorrelated investments. That way, if a market downturn affects one side of the portfolio, the noncorrelated assets from the other side of the portfolio can supply your income.

BELOW MEDIAN AND ABOVE MEDIAN BOND RETURN ENVIRONMENTS (1927-2016)

	Bellow Median Bond Return Enviroments Average Return	Above Median Bond Return Enviroments Average Return	Overall Period Average Return
Long Term Gov't Bonds	1.87%	9.00%	5.43%
Large Cap Stocks	11.43%	9.84%	10.63%
FIA	4.42%	7.55%	5.98%
60/40 (Stocks & Bonds)	7.60%	9.50%	8.55%
60/20/20 (Stocks, Bonds & FIA)	8.12%	9.21%	8.66%
60/40 (Bonds & FIA)	8.63%	8.92%	8.77%

Professor Roger Ibbotson illustrates in his whitepaper (referenced in the above chart) the diversification benefits of utilizing a fixed index annuity in conjunction with other asset classes to reduce volatility and risk in a rising interest rate environment while maintaining growth potential.[25]

In a low-interest rate environment, allocating more funds to traditional fixed income investments has meant taking on unnecessary interest rate risks if interest rates begin to rise. Think of it this way: say you buy a bond today, paying 3 percent interest, but next year, the same bond might pay 4 percent. If you must sell your 3 percent bond that year, you'll have to sell it at a discount because of the more attractive, higher interest-paying bonds available.

In addition to interest rate risks, bonds face default risks— even the highest quality bonds can default (at one time, the Lehman Brothers bonds were rated very highly). By using a fixed index annuity that credits your contract based on 75 percent of the S&P 500's gains, gains are locked in every two years and protect your principal. In short, you can avoid the default and interest rate risk of traditional fixed income investments. Also, there's the possibility of achieving a higher rate of return due to the historical returns of the stock market versus fixed income products. This isn't to say that fixed income or bonds are obsolete, but you may want to investigate diversifying with these types of fixed income alternatives. After all, the age-old rule of diversification cannot be overlooked.

The point here with the flexible withdrawal strategy is that we generate income from whichever investments perform the best, locking in our gains periodically as we take withdrawals. But, if those investments experienced losses, we would be able to shift withdrawals to those defensive tools that were either performing well during market downturns or experiencing little to no loss. Such defensive tools include bonds, commodities (gold) or even guaranteed products (fixed index annuities).

Independence

One more thing to keep in mind as you are evaluating various retirement income strategies and the products therein should be your advisor's access to tools. Not all financial professionals have the same licensing, and even among those who do, the range of companies they work with greatly affects their ability to access the right tools for the job.

Many soon-to-be-retirees switch financial advisors as they prepare for the next stage of their lives (or, for some, they seek a financial advisor for the first time). Inevitably, as they search for the right financial professional, they find certain advisors avoid some of the strategies altogether, which could be due to advisor bias or simply because of licensing or employment restrictions.

For instance, there are hundreds of options when it comes to annuities. In the same sense, there are numerous products and product types in the stock or bond market, and the quality of these products can vary widely due to their rates or the strength of the carrier offering the product.

Once, I had a couple visit me to get a second opinion on the financial tools they had been sold a couple of years earlier. They were working with a major national firm with offices across the country. This firm, however, focused its insurance offerings largely on the proprietary products they offered.

The couple purchased a fixed annuity paying 2.5 percent per year with a ten-year surrender charge period and no guarantees that the interest crediting rate wouldn't decrease. Had they worked with an independent advisor with the ability to shop amongst carriers, circumstances might have been different. They might have arranged for a 3.5 percent fixed rate annuity with a five-year surrender charge period and a guarantee the rate would never change.

You may also see the same with fixed index annuities. One company may offer a 20 percent participation rate in the S&P 500, while another highly rated carrier offers 50 percent or more.

One thing to keep in mind is how the "financial planning" world (really the brokerage world) was founded on securities offerings, such as stocks, bonds, mutual funds, variable annuities, etc., which large national financial firms often developed in-house and sold to their clients. Today, very few national financial firms sell proprietary products, but they still almost exclusively focus on at-risk investment offerings. At the same time, they ignore and poo-poo fixed and fixed index annuities altogether because of the enormous amount of income that has been generated through their investment partners over the years.

We are beginning to see a shift in the industry, where more national firms are offering products with better guarantees. However, their range of options is always limited due to the agreements they have with their product partners. For instance, say an advisor is with Big Box Megabrokerage firm. Big Box Megabrokerage might have what is called a "revenue-sharing agreement" with the Lifetime Moneycorp Inc. company. When Big Box Megabrokerage's advisors sell a Lifetime Moneycorp Inc. product, Lifetime Moneycorp shares a portion of that revenue back to Big Box Megabrokerage and sometimes to the advisor—something commonly known as a "kickback."

The reason for this is obvious: Lifetime Moneycorp wants to incentivize agents to sell its product. Who do you think ultimately pays for that kickback? That's right—whoever is buying the product. And whoever is buying could pay twice, in a certain sense. Not only are they subsidizing the revenue-sharing system upfront with their purchase, but they are also at risk of opportunity costs if their agent passes over better products to sell the Lifetime Moneycorp product (which was more lucrative to the agent).

INCOME PLANNING

As Dr. Pfau said in the *Retire With Purpose*™ podcast, "It's advisors who are just licensed on one side that I think increasingly recognize the value of both, and you are finding more advisors today who are more comfortable looking at both the insurance and the investment worlds to build a more holistic plan."

To get the best range of options, you will want to work with a truly independent advisor who is not tied to a national brokerage firm. This provides you access to shop the universe of options available.

Social Security Planning[26]

YOUR FULL RETIREMENT AGE

Year of Birth	Full Retirement Age
1937 or earlier	65
1938	65 and 2 months
1939	65 and 4 months
1940	65 and 6 months
1941	65 and 8 months
1942	65 and 10 months
1943-1954	66
1955	66 and 2 months
1956	66 and 4 months
1957	66 and 6 months
1958	66 and 8 months
1959	66 and 10 months
1960 or later	67

During your retirement income planning, don't overlook Social Security! Your retirement income strategy is made up of many puzzle pieces, and, for most Americans, their Social Security income will be a primary source of retirement income. Despite this, it is one that is often undervalued. Too often, this is because people make quick decisions regarding Social Security, overlooking strategies and costing themselves thousands and even hundreds of thousands of dollars. Let's look at the real value of your Social Security benefit so you can see what I mean. If your benefit is $1,000 per month, it would take at least $300,000 in private assets to generate that kind of income over the course of retirement—which only allows you to withdraw 4 percent and doesn't factor in market volatility or the numerous tax advantages afforded to Social Security income. Now, you wouldn't go out and blow $300,000 without doing your research, so why would you do so with your Social Security benefit?

Simply hitting retirement age and filing for your benefit without doing any research is akin to just that—it's irresponsible. Social Security filing and benefit options are regularly evolving, so whatever strategy you have today may need to change by the time you get to retirement. For instance, at one time, you could collect spousal benefits while your spouse was still delaying benefits. This allowed you to both file under your own income records later in life when deferral credits had fattened up their monthly checks.

In the Bipartisan Budget Act of 2015, which President Barack Obama signed into law, this "loophole" closed, but when it was popular, Social Security beneficiaries collected essentially extra benefits over and above typical filing strategies, often adding tens of thousands of extra dollars to a retiree's bottom line. There are unique circumstances for divorcees and widows as well that may or may not be closed in the future, and many times, these benefits are overlooked.[27]

INCOME PLANNING

The basic rules for Social Security are that the agency calculates your monthly benefit based on your income earnings during your career, your life expectancy and what age you file relative to your full retirement age. Your full retirement age or FRA may be sixty-six to sixty-seven, depending on the year you were born. You can file for your benefits as early as sixty-two and have your monthly check reduced from what it would be at FRA. Or, you can delay filing to age seventy, for which your monthly check will increase from what it would have been if you filed at FRA. Of course, even if you have a sizeable gap in your career—a common scenario for many whose careers were largely domestic or based on volunteering in their communities—you can file to receive spousal benefits or up to 50 percent of what your spouse qualifies for at their FRA.[28]

Yet, these are not universal rules. You may have special circumstances if your spouse died or if you are caring for a minor or disabled child of a divorced or deceased spouse. It pays to poke around and be sure you know all the rules and exceptions that pertain to your unique situation.

For instance, a sixty-year-old widow who was struggling to make ends meet after losing her husband hadn't realized that she was eligible to file for a survivor Social Security benefit.[29] She learned about the special provisions that applied to her situation, allowing her to file for benefits immediately. She may have missed out on a few months of benefits, but once she filed, the extra monthly income she received changed her life. Where she was once struggling to make ends meet, she was now able to do things she couldn't before, like going out to eat with a group of longtime friends.

My mom was another case of a unique situation allowing for incredible Social Security planning opportunities. The Bipartisan Budget Act of 2015 may have eliminated special filing opportunities for married couples, but it left those same rules in place for divorcees, leading to some criticism of the government for "subsidizing divorce." When Mom reached her full retirement age (FRA), she could file for spousal benefits based on my father's (her ex-husband's) Social Security record, to the tune of approximately $1,100 per month. Had she filed for her own benefits, she would have received roughly $1,200 per month. By deciding to first file on my father's benefit, though, she could delay her own benefit and earn delayed filing credits to age seventy. Then, upon reaching age seventy, she could switch her filing to her own earnings record, giving her a $1,500 monthly check. That is a bigger check going into her pocket for the rest of her life.

MEET STEVE AND BARBARA

Steve and Barbara were retiring early from the same company at age sixty. Their company offered a variety of pension benefits. The most beneficial, after thorough analysis, was a ten-year, period-certain option guaranteeing all their income needs would be satisfied until age seventy. This allowed for a few different planning opportunities. One opportunity, and the most obvious, was their ability to get the highest monthly Social Security check by delaying filing to age seventy.

The second and less obvious opportunity was with their taxes. An often-overlooked feature of Social Security is that, since 1983, a portion of many retirees' Social Security benefits is subject to federal income taxes. Due to Social Security originally being an untaxed benefit altogether, many people forget things have changed. Depending on your income sources and their taxability, up to 85 percent of your Social Security benefits can be taxed during retirement.[30] With appropriate planning, however, you may be able to eliminate these taxes altogether, as Steve and Barbara did.

They retired with a substantial amount of pre-tax assets in their 401(k)s, which they would not require for retirement income needs. It essentially became an overblown emergency fund. Unfortunately, due to the required minimum distributions on 401(k)s, Steve and Barbara came across an issue. After age seventy-two (or age seventy-three for those who reached seventy-two after December 31, 2022), they would be forced to begin taking taxable distributions from their traditional retirement accounts, regardless of whether they needed the income. Failing to take RMDs could result in a 25 percent tax penalty of whatever the missed RMD is. But, as we looked down the road, we saw that Steve and Barbara's RMDs would push most of their Social Security income into a taxable range in addition to pushing them into higher marginal tax brackets.

Thankfully, with the passing of the SECURE Act in late 2019, the required minimum distribution age was pushed back to seventy-two, giving them over a decade before RMDs kicked in, allowing Steve and Barbara even more opportunity to create a tax-efficient retirement in their later years. They are using this period to convert most of their tax-deferred retirement dollars to after-tax retirement accounts, which will grow tax-free via Roth IRA conversions. Roth IRAs can grow tax-free without the requirement for distributions until the death of the owner. This almost eliminated the taxes Steve and Barbara would have paid on their Social Security benefits and minimized the amount of federal, state and local taxes they would pay over their lifetime. It may even save them on Medicare premiums over their lifetime by avoiding IRMAA (Income Related Monthly Adjustment Amount) penalties that they would be forced to pay if their income exceeded certain levels.[31]

It is worth noting that beginning in 2033, the age to begin taking RMDs will rise even further to seventy-five.

When it comes to Social Security planning, the rules are always changing. As you can see from the previous examples, though, there are many potential landmines and many opportunities to avoid them if you plan. If you view your retirement as a puzzle, you should see that Social Security is one very large piece!

Tax Planning

Another piece of your retirement puzzle that is often overlooked? The benefits of tax planning opportunities, particularly within your retirement income strategy. Too often, this is reduced to a single question: Which bucket of funds should you spend first—the taxable, tax-deferred or tax-free?

This isn't necessarily as easy of a question as it may seem. Many financial advisors recommend that you spend the taxable dollars first to preserve the tax benefits of the tax-deferred and tax-free dollars.[32] However, this should not be generalized, as everyone is unique in this respect. There are more factors we must consider before deciding how to approach assets with different tax situations.

Our team worked with a couple who was lucky enough to diversify their tax dollars in such a way that they had substantial funds in each of these buckets. This allowed for planning opportunities many don't have when everything is largely in one bucket. For example, most often, retirees are highly concentrated in the tax-deferred bucket.

After projecting taxability both today and in the future—including potential penalties and taxation on Medicare and Social Security benefits—it made sense to use a blended withdrawal strategy, primarily aimed at minimizing their current and future tax obligations. We allocated the taxable dollars to their emergency fund, which we positioned to grow tax-deferred should they need the funds in the future. In the event an emergency never arises, the asset will pass tax-free to their heirs. We then took a blended income from their tax-deferred IRAs and tax-free Roth IRAs, as well as cash-value life insurance policies. This permitted us to level out RMDs over their lifetime, as well as minimize tax consequences today.

Retirement income planning isn't as simple as just throwing investments into a few accounts, setting up a regular distribution, and hoping things work out. There is much more involved than that if you want to have the confidence to spend during your retirement years.

> For more on this topic, check out the Podcast section of the Howard Bailey website and watch our video, "Retirement Planning, Step 6: Tax Planning":
>
> HOWARDBAILEY.COM/096

TAKEAWAYS, ACTIONS AND NOTES

What are your biggest takeaways from this chapter?

_____
_____
_____
_____
_____
_____
_____

What are three action steps that you should work on now?

1. _____

2. _____

3. _____

What are three action steps for later?

1. _____

2. _____

3. _____

INCOME PLANNING

NOTES:

CHAPTER FIVE

FLEXIBILITY PLANNING

I often say retirement is about income, not growth. Most of your life has been about growth—accumulation at all costs!—but in retirement, your focus must shift to income and making those funds last a lifetime. I reiterate these words regularly because today's retiree has been focused on nothing but growth their entire life. Turning those hard-earned assets into a regular income takes a major mental shift that most retirees struggle with.

I'm not saying you should ignore long-term growth during retirement. Many retirees will still be investing for the long term when they first retire. It ultimately comes down to prioritization. In retirement, your priorities shouldn't focus on growth or the returns on your money; your priority should be the return of your money—cash flow.

However, once you have satisfied your cash flow needs using one of the previous strategies, you can then begin structuring some of your remaining assets for long-term growth, which may be needed.

You want to adapt to an unknown future that may primarily involve playing defense against inflation eroding your spending power in addition to other unknowns you will encounter throughout retirement.

Planning is about controlling what we can and playing defense against the rest. Your emergency fund should be priority No. 1, followed by a reliable income strategy that lends you the confidence needed to spend during retirement and then the long-term growth of the funds you may need down the road to defend against the known unknowns as well as the unknown unknowns. Inflation will affect everyone differently and falls smack dab in the known unknown category, making it a good focus for our discussion around flexibility.

> *"There has been a seismic shift in retirement security from a time when many people could rely on a pension in retirement. Today, many Americans are facing a retirement crisis because they are at risk of running out of money in their retirement."*
>
> –Jason Fichtner, a senior fellow and head of the Retirement Income Institute and chief economist at the Bipartisan Policy Center.[33]

MEET LEE

Lee first walked into my office in 2010. Upon entering the conference room, I didn't even get a chance to sit down before he shared with me the outstanding job he had done saving for retirement. He said,

FLEXIBILITY PLANNING

"I'm fifty-two years old and have $740,000 saved for retirement." He shared with me that he had worked at the local gas company his entire career—I had guessed that much since he sported a shirt with their logo. Lee had been working as much overtime as he possibly could to maximize his 401(k) contributions year after year. He was already debt-free and headed to an early retirement with a goal of retiring at fifty-nine-and-one-half—a date he set because it was the earliest he thought he could access funds from his retirement account without a 10 percent tax penalty. He told me he didn't save his money so he could leave it behind; quite the contrary. He wanted to retire early and spend as much as possible every month, straight to the point of handing over his last dollar and writing a bad check right before they put a nail in the coffin.

Lee didn't have any children or a spouse to take over his life savings. He wanted to enjoy his retirement to the fullest and do things he was never able to do while sacrificing time during his employment. Of course, longevity risk was a real concern for him. In addition, how would we know how much he could spend month in and month out without being able to predict market activity? In this case, a guaranteed income strategy was perfect. It provided Lee with a guaranteed income, which he could not outlive on a portion of his life savings while leaving the rest for his flexibility bucket. Inflation was a real concern of his; he had longevity in his blood and had a significant chance of being retired longer than he worked!

> **LONGEVITY RISK IS THE RISK THAT THE AMOUNT OF MONEY AN INDIVIDUAL SAVES FOR RETIREMENT MIGHT NOT BE ENOUGH TO SUSTAIN THEM, DUE TO INCREASED LIFE EXPECTANCY.**

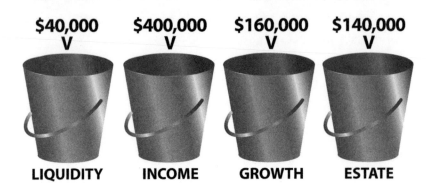

At Howard Bailey, we recommend setting aside a certain percentage of a portfolio purely for long-term growth to defend against unknowns, such as inflation, based on many factors that vary from person to person. In the case of Lee, we decided to set 40 percent of the assets in his income strategy aside for flexibility. We separated his assets to focus on two competing purposes: return of his money, or income, and return on his money, or growth. Since Lee had about $740,000 in total assets to work with, we allotted about $400,000 to income-generating assets with the aim of generating $20,000 a year, and then we put about $160,000 aside for future inflation protection. This left us with $140,000 to set aside for other potential needs and liabilities, such as health care expenses, and $40,000 for liquidity or emergency purposes.

The amount anyone sets aside for both income and growth will be determined by several different assumptions each client and advisor will need to discuss. The numbers listed in Lee's example are general guidelines based on historical market returns and inflation.

FLEXIBILITY PLANNING

As a result, these buckets could be nearly depleted over the course of retirement, allowing for annual inflation increases along the way, but since we implemented a guaranteed lifetime income strategy, he would never run out of income even if he depleted 100 percent of his assets. These numbers are not precise because interest, inflation rate estimates and market considerations are, at best, assumptions and also because the spending habits of a retiree will change over time.

My college finance professor referred to these years as the "Go-Go," "Slow-Go" and "No-Go" years—meaning most retirees will see a reduction in discretionary spending over the span of their retirement, though they will also see an increase in spending on such things as health care. For instance, later in retirement, you may not be traveling, driving or golfing as much as you used to. You may also downsize and potentially even possess one car instead of two.

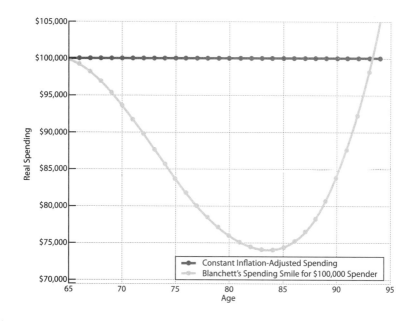

The research backs this up: older individuals spend less yet feel more content in that as they deal with health issues, experience the loss of a partner or simply age, their interest in certain activities might decrease. This naturally leads to less spending on those activities.[35] Furthermore, retirees with higher retirement expenses at the onset of retirement will be affected even less than those retirees with less retirement expenses at the onset of retirement. This is because retirees with higher expenses at the beginning of retirement typically have a larger budget for discretionary spending than those of retirees with lower expenses. However, this doesn't mean the past will be representative of the future, hence inflation being an unknown known and demanding a flexible strategy to adapt.

> For more information on retiree spending patterns and the relative impact of inflation, check out my *Retire With Purpose*™ podcast with Dr. David Blanchett, head of retirement research at Morningstar Investment Management, where we discuss his groundbreaking research into this topic:
>
> HOWARDBAILEY.COM/055

Finding the Right Inflation Hedge

Once you have determined the appropriate size of your flexibility bucket, it's time to find appropriate investments. You typically want to avoid conservative fixed income products as inflation hedges. They will most likely pay a rate of return at or below the rate of inflation. Instead, you want your inflation hedge to grow faster than inflation and be composed of a diversified investment portfolio.

FLEXIBILITY PLANNING

Despite what you may have heard on the latest radio or television advertisements, gold hasn't always been the best inflation hedge—particularly in the hyperinflation era of the late '70s and early '80s when gold inflated in tandem with overall inflation.[36] The same is true for dividend-paying stocks.[37] The truth is that there are too many variables over too much time for us to define one specific inflation hedge that will perform the same forever.

Inflation doesn't affect you overnight. Tomorrow, you will likely pay the same amount for the gallon of milk or carton of eggs at the store as you did today. Yet, inflation will eventually start to work against you, especially if your expenses are mostly non-discretionary. That gallon of milk and carton of eggs may cost the same tomorrow, but what about in a year? Five years? Ten? This is another reason you will be taking the most amount of risk with your inflation-hedging assets. These funds have time to go through the various ups and downs of at-risk markets that your other funds cannot afford, as you may need them for emergencies, income or health care costs.

The obvious result of inflation is having to pay more to fill the gas tank, buy a gallon of milk or even get a haircut—overall, an increase in your general cost of living. Inflation can become a real concern, which is why President Ronald Reagan said, "Inflation is as violent as a mugger, as frightening as an armed robber and as deadly as a hit man."

The simplest form of inflation protection is finding ways to profit from the increasing prices of goods and services. The argument goes that stocks are claims on real assets, such as land, plants and equipment, which appreciate in value as overall prices increase. This fact is historically supported in general; over thirty-year periods, stock returns have been virtually unaffected by the inflation rate.[38] This isn't always the case over shorter periods of time. Stocks have historically done well against inflation when the inflation rate is in the 2 to 3 percent range but have faltered when inflation has exceeded 3 percent in the short term.[39]

Investments in the U.S. Capital Markets (1927-2016)[40]

So, while stocks can provide great long-term inflation protection, you may want to also diversify into alternative investments to ensure proper inflation protection, especially if we see periods of hyperinflation. When it comes to your assets that are aimed at protecting against inflation, you will want to avoid the bond market. The exception is for **Treasury Inflation Protection Securities (TIPS)**, which are Treasury bonds whose principal value increases with inflation and decreases with deflation and returns the adjusted principal or original principal (whichever is greater) to the investor upon maturity.[41] This is one of the most conservative inflation-hedging options available to your portfolio.

Gold and other commodities also perform well in periods of high and increasing inflation, but the results have not been so spectacular in the long term. For instance, gold has only returned a little less than one percentage point per year over that of the inflation rate in the past few centuries. That doesn't mean commodities don't have a place as an inflation hedge; you just might want to include investments in companies that will profit from increases in commodity prices, such as miners, drillers, storage facilities and transporters of commodities. Real estate exposure can be another effective inflation hedge as part of a diversified portfolio.

> Treasury inflation protected securities (tips) refer to a treasury security that is indexed to inflation in order to protect investors from the negative effects of inflation.

To round out your long-term growth portfolio for inflation protection, you should consider investing internationally.

Roth Conversion Opportunities

By segmenting our portfolios with different risk levels and asset types, we usually find ourselves presented with more tax planning opportunities than if all investments are in the same proverbial pot.

One tax crunch many retirees find themselves in is with their IRA and 401(k) assets. As I've discussed previously regarding RMDs, even if you don't need income from your traditional IRA, you may find yourself in a tricky tax scenario. Remember, traditional IRAs are tax-deferred, not tax-free. One way to avoid potentially being pushed into a higher tax bracket in later retirement is to pay taxes on those IRA assets now and then allow them to grow tax-free in a **Roth IRA**.

First, let's unpack the basic difference between traditional and Roth IRAs. One of the ways I like to describe the difference is by using a common complaint I hear at family gatherings. Many in my extended family are farmers, and they have a lot of experience with working hard, only to see the fruits of their labors diminished by weather, insects, disease, foraging animals and taxes. A common lament is wishing they could pay taxes on their seed, then grow their crops and sell the harvest tax-free. This is really the difference between a traditional IRA and a Roth IRA.

> A roth ira is an individual retirement plan that bears many similarities to the traditional ira. The biggest distinction between the two is how they're taxed. Roth iras are funded with after-tax dollars; the contributions are not tax deductible. But when you start withdrawing funds, qualified distributions are tax free.

With a traditional IRA, you get a deduction for the taxes you would normally pay today, and it grows tax-deferred—until you start withdrawing money from your IRA. Then, you will pay a full income tax on your original contributions and any gains you made over the last several decades of investing.

Just to make sure he gets his cut, Uncle Sam has a rule that, after you turn seventy-two, you must withdraw at least a certain percentage (based on your life expectancy) of your account every year. These are the RMDs we outlined earlier, the required withdrawals that can force you to not only pay more in federal, state and local taxes but also on your Social Security benefits (and potentially even higher costs of Medicare premiums due to IRMAA).

By contrast, with a Roth IRA, you pay income taxes on the money that goes into the account. You won't pay taxes on any qualified distributions you withdraw, which means both your contributions and any gains they have made will come out of the account tax-free. The money that has already been taxed won't have required minimum distributions. If there is money left in the account when you die, your heirs inherit those funds tax-free.

Few people would choose to convert their traditional IRA to a Roth as a lump sum. Can you imagine the tax consequences of paying income taxes on hundreds and thousands of dollars all at once? Converting smaller portions (just enough to fill up your current tax bracket) over a decade or so can greatly decrease the impact of traditional IRA RMDs on your taxable situation.

One opportunity to convert funds may be during a dip in the market. While your IRA assets are negatively affected, it might make sense to convert the depressed assets from your traditional IRA to a Roth IRA. You will pay less in ordinary income taxes today while the value is depressed and then will be able to take advantage of having a larger tax-free value when the market rebounds. This takes your new Roth funds to greater heights. I did this with our personal IRA accounts near the bottom of the market in 2020 amidst the COVID-19 pandemic.

Another unique opportunity has presented itself in the Tax Cuts and Jobs Act of 2017 (TCJA). After Congress passed the TCJA, Roth conversions essentially went on sale. We previously recommended you make Roth conversions in the 15 percent brackets and below while also doing the same in the 25 percent bracket if you have substantial tax-deferred retirement accounts and/or taxable income in retirement.

However, the TCJA shifted the goal line. Those who were in the 15 percent bracket moved to the 12 percent bracket, the 25 percent moved to the 22 percent bracket and the 24 percent bracket covered married couples filing jointly all the way up to $383,900 in taxable income.* (*Brackets are adjusted for inflation annually and may be higher than those referenced in this book. As of 2024, the brackets listed here are up to date.) This means that to fill up your bracket with money for a partial Roth conversion, you may have a lot more latitude to convert funds than what you would have in previous years. Keep in mind, though, that these income tax brackets may only last until 2026 when the rules will "sunset" back to inflation-adjusted 2017 levels. In fact, David McKnight argues, on episode #114 of the *Retire With Purpose*™ podcast (https://retirewithpurpose.com/podcast/), that we have more certainty regarding higher taxes in the future than potentially any other time throughout modern history.

The following chart shows a side-by-side comparison of how the 2017 marginal tax rates for single and married filers compare to the rates and income limits of the 2024 rates. Keep in mind that it's not just the monetary limits that are changed (albeit temporarily), but the actual percentage rates, as well.

You might think your CPA or tax preparer should be all over this opportunity, but you could be wrong.

MARGINAL INCOME TAX BRACKETS

2017				2024		
RATE	SINGLE FILERS	MARRIED FILING JOINTLY		RATE	SINGLE FILERS	MARRIED FILING JOINTLY
10%	$0-$9,325	$0-$18,650		10%	$0-$11,600	$0-$23,200
15%	$9,326-$37,950	$18,651-$75,900		12%	$11,601-$47,150	$23,201-$94,300
25%	$37,951-$91,900	$75,901-$153,100		22%	$47,151-$100,525	$94,301-$201,050

28%	$91,901-$191,650	$153,101-$233,350		24%	$100,526-$191,950	$201,051-$383,900
33%	$190,651-$416,700	$233,351-$416,700		32%	$191,951-$243,725	$383,901-$487,450
35%	$416,701-$418,400	$416,701-$470,700		35%	$243,726-$609,350	$487,451-$731,200
39.6%	$418,400+	$470,700+		37%	$609,351+	$731,201+

MEET MICHAEL AND PAULA

I once had a CPA, Michael, who came in to visit with our team for a second set of eyes on his personal investments. He was a fairly successful entrepreneur—he started, grew and ultimately sold his accounting practice at a relatively young age. After selling his practice in his early fifties, he decided to retire.

His wife, Paula, was still working part-time, and together, they had minimal expenses due to becoming debt-free during Michael's working career. Essentially, they could live off her income. Paula enjoyed her job and didn't mind bridging the gap they had until they qualified to receive Social Security, at which point they planned to file early and live a comfortable retirement almost exclusively off their Social Security paychecks. He enjoyed managing his own investments and did a pretty decent job.

While the accounts were invested quite aggressively with little diversification, it was OK. They didn't ever plan to spend the funds and were holding a substantial emergency fund just in case. In addition, they kept their investing expenses low, using low-cost index funds. Many retirees don't want to have to worry about their money or think about the day-to-day movements of the stock market—Michael was an exception. He saw it as an exciting opportunity and shared with me that he spent an hour or two every day evaluating each of his holdings and studying the markets. It was fun for him.

When we asked to see a tax return, he seemed bewildered, saying he obviously had that under control. He was trained in tax planning, for goodness' sake. He went on to share with us that their tax bill was negligible, as their life savings were stuffed away in tax-deferred retirement accounts—largely his IRA from his working years. He was very proud of the fact that they maintained income in what was the 15 percent tax bracket at the time despite technically being millionaires. The reality was that he was doing what most CPAs do: looking back at the previous tax year and using their tax return as a scorecard to see how well they did. It's not the CPA's fault. It stems back to how they are trained and graded year after year by their clients. This is a viewpoint that is based on looking in the tiny rearview mirror instead of the huge windshield in front of you; the taxes headed your way are the bugs splattering on it.

This CPA had accumulated over $1 million in retirement accounts and about twenty years away from being forced to take distributions out of them—when he didn't even need the money. As aggressively as he was investing, that million dollars could double twice over the next twenty years in a good market, turning into almost $4 million by the time they were seventy-two. Their RMDs would start at roughly $150,000 and only increase from there. This would take them from what is currently the 10 percent bracket all the way to the 25 percent bracket and beyond—their RMDs would likely get larger as their IRA grew and life expectancy shortened. It would force them to pay taxes on Social Security benefits that were previously tax-free when they first turned them on at sixty-two and potentially increase their Medicare premiums, not to mention increasing their federal, state and local taxes each year.

After Michael redirected himself to look ahead, he and Paula structured a tax strategy that would keep them in a 15 percent tax bracket and potentially convert as much as half of their tax-deferred traditional retirement accounts to tax-free Roth accounts. With the lower and wider tax brackets created by the TCJA, they might even be able to justify converting all their tax-deferred savings into tax-free savings by converting larger amounts at lower rates, creating a truly tax-free retirement. Keep in mind that this tax sale is slated to last for a limited time. These rates are set to expire after 2025, and changes could happen sooner. This is one sale you don't want to let pass you by, or you'll be paying for it for the rest of your life.

Watch Your Expenses

Another opportunity in the flexibility bucket and really for your entire portfolio is to minimize your ongoing fees and expenses—a simple way to put more growth on the table and money in your pocket. It is now easier than ever to invest in the market. Heck, you don't even need a broker anymore. You can hop online and start trading stocks or mutual funds completely on your own. As a result, costs to investors have fallen dramatically. Now, I don't want to say that cost is everything. **Hedge funds** that charge "two-and-twenty" (2 percent per year and 20 percent of annual profits) can still beat the returns in the most inexpensive mutual funds. On the other hand, access to these types of funds is reserved for the ultra-wealthy, leaving the rest of us stuck with more traditional market-based investments—typically with less annual returns and dramatically lower costs than ever before.

> A hedge fund is basically a fancy name for an investment partnership. It's the marriage of a professional fund manager, who can often be known as the general partner, and the investors, sometimes known as the limited partners, who pool their money together into the fund.

One area where the financial services industry finds the most fees? Mutual fund products of days past. The reality is that most investors don't know what they are actually paying in fees and expenses. In fact, a study conducted by the United States Government Accountability Office shows that many people do not understand the fee information provided by their 401(k) plan. Additionally, 41 percent of participants incorrectly believe that they do not pay any 401(k) plan fees.[42] The reality is that the fees in your mutual funds inside of your 401(k) are significant.

Not long ago, I had a retiree, Don, come to me for an independent scan of the annual fees and expenses he was paying his advisor. He worked with one of the most prestigious registered investment advisory firms in the country at the time, where every dime he had was invested in mutual funds to the tune of $3,300,000. His investment advisory fees were 1 percent per year, in addition to the mutual fund expenses that averaged 1.36 percent per year (a bit lower than the average mutual fund fees we were seeing at the time). That brought his total costs to nearly $80,000 per year, though changes were rarely, if ever, made to the mutual fund holdings themselves. His portfolio contained some of the same mutual funds my two-year-old son had in his **529 plan** at the time, with just a few thousand dollars. Why would someone with more than $3 million dollars invest the same way as a two-year-old?

> A 529 plan provides tax advantages when saving and paying for higher education. There are two major types: prepaid tuition plans and savings plans. Prepaid tuition plans allow the plan holder to pay for the beneficiary's tuition and fees at designated institutions in advance. Savings plans are tax-advantaged investment vehicles, similar to iras.

The following chart illustrates the compounded effect of different fee levels, from a 1 percent fee to a 3 percent fee. The fees you pay matter and add up to potentially millions of dollars over time, much more than the few dollars you shell out for other expenses.

There comes a time when you can transition to the institutionally managed world, the one that used to be reserved for the ultra-wealthy, much like the hedge-fund world. This is the way large institutions and trust funds manage their wealth. Do you think a multibillion-dollar trust fund would invest in mutual funds? Of course not. Instead, they go to third-party money managers who assist them in managing their funds in accounts, holding securities specifically for their goals in mind. These investors place their money in stocks, bonds, index funds and other individual holdings they will own themselves rather than a pooled mutual fund investment composed of hundreds or thousands of people across the country. This type demands complete transparency when it comes to not only their holdings but their fees and expenses, as well.

Mutual Funds

One of the reasons brokers enjoy mutual funds is due to the lack of transparency regarding fees and expenses; it's much easier to keep clients invested when they don't see the annual fees and expenses coming directly out of their investment portfolio. Not only can you not see and feel the basic expenses (known as 12b-1 fees), but some expenses aren't even required to be disclosed, such as transaction costs. Every time something is bought and sold in a mutual fund, it is passed through a brokerage, and the fund pays a commission, which is not disclosed as part of the fund's annual expenses. Mutual fund expense ratios are typically between 0.25 percent and 1 percent of your investment in the fund per year.[43] With a third-party managed account, known as a separately or unified managed account, you have not only complete transparency in your exact holdings, but you can also see every fee and expense in your account as long as your money isn't pooled into investment vehicles, such as mutual funds. If you don't feel like your broker is performing well, you can at least see what the underperformance is costing you.

Another drag a mutual fund can place on your annual returns includes taxes. According to Morningstar, the median ten-year tax-cost ratio for all U.S. stock funds was higher—1.49 percent.[44] When purchasing a mutual fund, you are not purchasing the individual stocks inside of the fund. Instead, you are buying into the net asset value of the fund itself. This comes along with unrealized tax liabilities of the individual holdings inside of the fund, which, when realized, will be passed onto you. Many investors experienced the downside of this during the tech bubble of the 2000s and the 2008 financial crisis, which is worth revisiting.

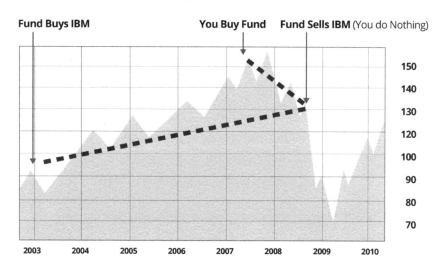

If you were to purchase a mutual fund owning IBM stock after the major run-up in mutual funds leading up to the financial crisis, say in 2007, you would have experienced a loss in value of your original investment following the 2008 market crash. However, since you purchased a fund with an unrealized gain, then that gain was passed onto you when it was sold, even though you didn't sell anything.

In contrast, if you invest in **separate or unified managed accounts**, you purchase the individual assets at whatever price they are at that time without undistributed tax liability—this results in much greater control over annual taxation and more money in your pocket over time.

Fees and Taxes

I don't want to understate the importance of fees and taxes when it comes to the growth side of your portfolio, but I also don't want to overstate them either—lest the tail wag the dog, so to speak. Sometimes, it might make sense to pay more for a sophisticated strategy with better potential or to take on additional taxable gains for an investment returning better after-tax returns than to pursue more tax-efficient investments.

> A separated managed account (sma) is a portfolio of assets managed by a professional investment firm. One or more portfolio managers are responsible for day-to-day investment decisions, supported by a team of analysts, operations and administrative staff.
>
> A unified managed account (uma) is a professionally managed private investment account that can include multiple types of investments all in a single account. Investments may include mutual funds, stocks, bonds and exchange traded funds. Unified managed accounts are often rebalanced on a specified schedule.

MEET TOM AND JANICE

Take, for instance, Tom and Janice. They were letting the tax tail wag the dog. They were 100 percent invested in municipal bonds to avoid taxes and fees. They could have received twice the rate of return on corporate bonds of similar quality and maturity. Although corporate bonds would have been taxable, their net return would be substantially higher than on tax-free municipal bonds—not to mention how shortsighted an investment strategy like that is when it comes to diversification. Again, while taxes are important, don't get blinded by the sales pitch—understand what the bottom line is for you personally before making any major financial decision. These are just other items to keep in the back of your mind while you are building the fiscal retirement home of your dreams!

Your Fiscal House

You can view your Purpose-Based Asset Allocation as a fiscal house, starting with the foundation. The foundation is the most important part of the house. In this case, it will consist of your emergency fund. Next, we have walls and the interior of the house representing your retirement income plan, which should be diverse. On the roof, you will find your growth plan, where we begin to play defense against the unknowns of the future. Just as your roof will face some punishment from nature, so will your growth plan. Lastly, we put a fence around your assets, like you would around your home, to protect and ensure they pass on to those you love, as planned via a comprehensive estate plan.

JOB **OPTIONAL**

TAKEAWAYS, ACTIONS AND NOTES

What are your biggest takeaways from this chapter?

_____
_____
_____
_____
_____
_____
_____

What are three action steps that you should work on now?

1. _____
2. _____
3. _____

What are three action steps for later?

1. _____
2. _____
3. _____

FLEXIBILITY PLANNING

NOTES:

CHAPTER SIX
ESTATE PLANNING

We may be ending our L.I.F.E. planning discussion with estate planning, but this doesn't mean you should hold off on this planning until the very end! Quite the contrary, this is a key area of your overall financial plan—leaving it unaddressed has led to some of the greatest retirement disasters I have seen throughout my career. Consequences range from forcing retirees back to work, losing substantial portions of legacies to taxes, damaging family relationships and even having whole estates default to unintended individuals.

Estate planning is the last piece of our L.I.F.E. plan, not because it lacks importance but because we must prioritize as we structure our retirement strategy. Some may not have the assets necessary to cover all areas of planning and will choose to accept that risk (such as long-term health care), while others may choose to extend their working career to cover every major risk and wish.

Without an emergency fund, your retirement may be very short-lived.

Without income, you don't have retirement.

Without inflation protection, you may not have the income you need later in life as the cost of living increases.

When it comes to estate planning, we are protecting assets as they pass on to our loved ones or protecting our estate from major health care expenses. Put another way: it comes down to disinheriting Uncle Sam and health care facilities to ensure there is something left for our beneficiaries in the end. This is a bigger priority for some than for others.

Many retirees put off thinking about the major health care risks they could face until it is too late. I see this most often with couples. It puts loved ones in a difficult situation at a very painful time in their lives.

MEET TOM AND MARGARET

There was once a widow, Margaret, who called our office in a panic following her first tax filing after the death of her husband the previous year. After more than sixty years of marriage, she had lost her husband, Tom, and was devastated. Not only was he the leader in their finances, but he also handled everything himself. There was limited communication between the couple regarding where their funds were, why they were there and what to do in case something happened to him. He did a great job of investing over the years and held a large portion of their assets in non-qualified fixed annuities due to his conservative nature. He owned these annuities for decades, benefitting from the tax deferral they offered—a feature I affectionately call "triple compounding," where the principal earns interest, the interest earns interest and the taxes that would normally be paid annually also earn interest.

ESTATE PLANNING

It worked great for Margaret and Tom, and by the time he died, the $500,000 they put in these fixed annuity contracts was worth over $1 million. When Tom passed away, Margaret went in to have a visit with their financial advisor, whom she had never met. At this point, Margaret was in her late eighties without a clue of what to do next. With Tom's passing, she became the sole owner of the annuities, and she could move or withdraw funds. Her advisor recommended taking a full withdrawal of the contracts and instead investing in a managed mutual fund portfolio, from which he would earn annual fees of 1.5 percent per year. By taking a lump sum distribution, all the gains in the annuities became taxable in a single year, costing her more than $150,000 in taxes on the annuity assets alone, not to mention taxes on Social Security and increases in Medicare premiums to boot.

If she hadn't taken a lump sum distribution, she could have withdrawn funds over time, distributing the taxable gains over an extended period.

Alternatively, she could have annuitized the contracts, received payments over a certain period (or even life) and still cut her tax bill to a fraction of the amount.

This is just one example of a tax travesty that occurred primarily because there wasn't a proper estate plan in place to communicate Tom's wishes about their contracts. Even so, an estate plan can only go so far—open dialogue involving both spouses in the planning conversation can go miles further.

This topic is incredibly important for women. Statistically speaking, women are more likely to be impacted by a lack of estate planning than men. The stories I share about legacy and estates often revolve around women because they are so often the ones left picking up the pieces. As David Bach, author of *Smart Women Finish Rich*, explained during our interview on the *Retire With Purpose*™ podcast (episode #17), most men will never know if the retirement plan they put in place ever works out, as their wives

will most likely outlive them and find out on their own. I hope this helps illustrate how terribly important it is for both spouses to have a basic understanding of where things are and why. Sometimes, it's not as dramatic as it was for Margaret, but it can still be just as painful for the surviving spouse.

> "Ladies… your retirement could be ten, fifteen, twenty years longer than the man in your life. That is a huge, huge issue, so you've got to prepare for that… And here's what I would tell you, ladies, and I would say this to the husbands, too:
>
> if you're married, imagine losing your spouse today and ask yourself, what do you need to know about the money tomorrow? And the answer is everything."
>
> ~David Bach

MEET BRENDA

Brenda came to visit us after the death of her husband, Michael. Prior to his death, she was told everything was set up and she would be fine. They had a couple hundred thousand dollars saved for retirement, along with a pension and Social Security income. They lived a happy and simple life. When Michael passed away, she lost the smaller of their two Social Security benefits—about a thousand dollars a month—and, unbeknownst to her, they had not selected survivors' benefits on her

ESTATE PLANNING

husband's pension. This meant $1,200 a month disappeared on top of her Social Security benefit. That left Brenda with just Michael's Social Security benefit ($1,500 per month) for a total monthly loss in income of almost 60 percent, or $2,200. Brenda's expenses were basically the same as before, but now she had about half as much income. She wanted to know how we could get her back to even. She would need to generate more than $25,000 a year from a $200,000 IRA, and she was only sixty-eight years old and in great health. Realistically, Brenda would likely face a dramatic lifestyle change or risk running out of money.

MEET BARRY AND MARY ELLEN

In another example of estate planning blunders, our team implemented a retirement plan for a couple who decided to retire early—both in their early sixties. Barry and Mary Ellen wanted to take Social Security benefits and ride off into the sunset—or, pretty close. They wanted to move to the sunshine state of Florida. They were both avid golfers, cyclists and health food nuts. Seriously, they never even accepted a coffee when they came in for a visit with our team. Nothing but water! As we walked them through our *Retire With Purpose*™ Framework, they chose not to address long-term care risks, explaining they were both in excellent health and none of their family members had ever needed nursing home care in the past. Well, as the financial advisor's disclaimer reads, past performance is no guarantee of future results.

Shortly after retirement, Barry was teeing up on his favorite course in Florida when he had a sudden and unexpected stroke. He had no history of heart conditions, nor did anyone in his family. To say it was unexpected would be an understatement. He was rushed to the hospital. His life and the lives of those in his family would be forever changed.

Barry's doctors told him he was never going to leave a high-care medical facility again. His stroke had been severe, causing memory issues that inhibited his ability to care for himself, along with difficulty speaking. Other than his memory and speech issues, Barry was in relatively good health—probably due to all the regular physical activity he was involved in. The doctors said he could live for years, but he would not be able to take care of himself.

Mary Ellen tried to take care of him at home and did so successfully for a period of time, but the toll on her own health became too much. To this day, Barry still spends most of his time in an assisted living facility, for which Medicare offers no coverage. After the stroke, Barry and Mary Ellen's health care expenses quickly rose to more than $40,000 per year. Their emergency fund was quickly depleted in the first few months of care, and their carefully crafted income strategy was maxed out with additional income needs distributed from their long-term growth assets.

Mary Ellen called us almost immediately after the incident to ask what could be done. Unfortunately, it was too late; she would either be forced to dramatically reduce her monthly spending or risk running out of money before she was seventy-five years old.

It didn't have to be this way, though; prior to Barry's stroke, they had plenty of assets and discretionary income to structure a long-term care strategy that would have provided the benefits necessary to cover these expenses, but they chose to take the risk.

Regardless of your current health status or your family history, long-term health care needs can cause financial devastation. For some families, their primary goal is to ensure they will never be a burden on their spouses or family members. For others, it is about preserving a legacy for the next generation or having the most choice regarding the quality of the facility they end up utilizing. Regardless of the purpose, it is always a need that should be evaluated during the planning process and planned for if possible. Not all estate planning blunders result in financial loss. Sometimes, they drop mental hardships on the next generation.

MEET MY GRANDFATHER, HOWARD

My grandfather fell into this latter category. He never wanted to address what would happen upon his death, not even the most basic estate planning or pre-planning for his funeral. This may not seem like that big of a deal, but it burdened my grandmother and their two children with a great deal of unnecessary stress. Being forced to pick out the simplest of things, such as what my grandfather would wear and what type of casket to purchase, were just a couple extra things that had to be added to his loved ones' plates upon his death. It could have easily been avoided by not just pre-paying his funeral expenses but pre-planning the funeral as well. It may not seem like much, but whatever can be done to lessen the burden and the number of decisions that need to be made upon death can make all the difference in the world.

MEET LISA

The lack of attention to simple beneficiary designations on policies and paperwork can have a huge impact on the children you leave behind as well. I once met with a woman named Lisa, who became the financial power of attorney for her father while he was still living. She opened investment accounts at a local bank to invest some of her father's cash when he reached his mid-nineties. The not-so-good news: Lisa neglected to designate specified beneficiaries on this account prior to his death. On the other hand, her father had already finalized a will designating her as the sole beneficiary of the estate. She was one of three siblings, but she assumed the responsibility of caring for her dad in his old age, while her other two siblings remained estranged and had no relationship with their father. Upon the father's death, the will directed the courts to pass all assets on to his daughter, but her siblings contested the will. As a result, the assets were not distributed for months due to litigation.

Ultimately, the courts fell back on the state "default" laws, distributing the account amongst all three children—against their father's wishes. Lisa told me that while she didn't have a fantastic relationship with her siblings prior to their father's death, after his death, they would most likely never speak again. The siblings felt she had coerced her father into making her the sole beneficiary of the estate. The drama could have been avoided with proper beneficiary designations.

The Importance of Probate

Many families overlook the fact that your beneficiary designations will bypass **probate**, while your will is a probate document directing assets that are not designated by beneficiary.

Essentially, your will is a letter to the judge, but it can be contested upon death. Proper beneficiary designations might have salvaged whatever relationship she had with her siblings and, at the very least, kept these assets out of the court—saving thousands of dollars in attorney fees along the way.

> Probate is a legal process in which a will is reviewed to determine whether it is valid and authentic.
>
> Probate also refers to the general administering of a deceased person's will or the estate of a deceased person without a will.

It's important to plan for what you want to happen to your assets after you're gone. One component of this includes the need to be able to have discussions with your loved ones about your wishes while you still can.

For some families, this is an easy, open and ongoing discussion. For others, it may be best to schedule a formal occasion to discuss planning. In my observation, though, the families who are kept most up-to-date and in the loop about estate planning are the ones who make it through the passing of the older generation most intact. Part of this is because shedding light on factors such as who will execute the will or who inherits the house from a parent face-to-face is often easier for siblings than finding out that so-and-so will be handling the estate transfer after the fact. Truly, planning early and being open about it can preserve much more than just a monetary legacy.

Basic Documents

As you can see, estate planning isn't all about working with a qualified estate planning attorney to structure appropriate documentation. It's about much more than just having the right paperwork in place. This is not to say these important documents should be overlooked in any way—quite the contrary. Your basic estate planning documents will be the foundation of your overall estate planning strategy. Yet, the degree of an estate's complexity can vary greatly from one family to the next, depending on their wishes, family structure and the size of the estate itself. Most families are able to get their needs covered through minor legal fees, and, in many cases, these documents can be completed inexpensively online rather than with a local estate planning attorney. When my wife and I had our first child, we didn't have substantial savings or business entities. Consequently, we just needed some basic estate planning. I hopped online and knocked out the most vital documents at minimal cost. As our business grew along with our savings, things became more complicated, and we needed to hire an estate planning attorney. However simple or complex your situation, you will need the basics at a minimum. Basics that should cover almost every family include a last will and testament, powers of attorney and a living will.

Last Will and Testament

Your last will and testament is essentially a catch-all document designating how you would like your property and assets distributed upon your death. Essentially, this is a letter to the probate judge. It will assist in directing assets without beneficiary designations attached to them to pass on according to your wishes. A will also designates an executor to ensure what you have specified will be carried out, in addition to naming guardians for any minor children you may have.

Powers of Attorney

Powers of attorney can be divided into two basic categories: health care and financial power of attorney. It is often a good idea to split these powers between individuals to avoid any potential conflicts of interest. A financial power of attorney allows you to designate someone to manage the financial decisions of your estate if you are unable to do so yourself. A health care power of attorney allows you to designate someone to make medical decisions on your behalf if you can't make them for yourself. Personally, I designated my father as my health care power of attorney and my wife as my financial power of attorney. I didn't want my wife to have to make difficult medical decisions that were in our family's best financial and psychological interest, but I knew my father could make these difficult decisions if he had to.

Living Will

A living will, also sometimes referred to as a health care proxy, ensures your wishes regarding medical care are followed in the event you become terminally ill and need to be on a life support system. A living will is only applicable if you are terminally ill or permanently unconscious. For this reason, it is wise to have both a living will and a designated health care power of attorney. A health care power of attorney will be responsible for managing health care decisions that may result from a temporary state of unconsciousness or inability to communicate, but not necessarily direct major decisions if you are terminally ill, in a permanently vegetative state or experiencing another end-stage condition. In some states, the living will and health care powers of attorney are combined into a single document that may also cover other various matters, such as the designation of a primary physician, desires regarding the donation of body organs and whom you would like appointed as your legal guardian if the need arises.

Trust

The preceding documents took care of my family's needs until the size of our estate grew to the point that I had greater concerns regarding the control of assets beyond the grave. Not only do I have to plan for my personal estate, but my wife and I must tie up the details pertaining to the various business entities we own and operate. As a result, we structured a revocable living trust.

While most individuals can simply use proper beneficiary designation in place of a trust to ensure assets avoid probate, families often use trusts to avoid probate. For our family, we had greater concerns regarding control over substantial financial and business assets passing to our children at a young age. The trust allowed us to establish goals and incentives for our children to gain control over the assets they would be left with in the case of our death—including educational, income and age earmarks for distribution. Sometimes, this is referred to as a goal-based trust.

The most common error with a revocable trust is keeping it funded in the first place. All assets that are intended to become part of the trust upon death should be owned by the trust prior to death, if possible. Otherwise, they will still become probateable upon death. While it is not necessary to have a lawyer involved to establish a trust, this document is typically only a requirement for more complex estate planning situations, which may be best handled via legal counsel.

A trust is a legal framework that allows an entity, such as a person or bank, to hold assets and transfer them from a trustor or grantor to the trustee. In our legal system, these can be revocable, meaning the trustor retains control over the assets during their lifetime, or irrevocable, meaning they can't get them out once the trustor puts them in. Trusts can be used to pass on money to minors, holding the assets until the child comes of age, or they can even be used to put other stipulations on the beneficiaries. Trusts can come in particularly handy for blended families, families with special needs children who will need care or families with specific charitable goals.

ESTATE PLANNING

MEET ROBERT AND HELEN

An example of someone who greatly benefited from a trust structure was a couple who had nearly $2 million in a single bank stock. Robert and Helen had a total net worth of just under $3 million. They relied on the dividend income from that stock to pay their bills in retirement but recognized they were taking a great deal of risk due to this highly concentrated holding. They didn't know what else to do. They inherited the bank stock decades prior, and it had appreciated greatly over time, with unrealized gains of over $1 million. If they were to sell the stock and diversify, the tax hit would cost them so much of their net worth that they would no longer be able to generate dividends at the same level moving forward to cover their expenses. They had no children and planned to pass all their assets to various charities. We worked with an attorney to establish a charitable trust, allowing them to contribute the stock to the trust.

Once inside the trust, Robert and Helen could liquidate and diversify the concentrated stock position without tax consequences. In addition, due to the nature of their trust with their favorite charities as beneficiaries, they would receive a charitable deduction they could use against their taxable income going into the future. This allowed them to gain much greater peace of mind. By pursuing the diversification and structure of a REAL income strategy, they could pick up tax deductions while still living, as opposed to tax benefits that would only benefit their estate after death.

MEET DAN AND JOANNA

In another instance, we worked with a couple who had a special needs daughter. She was their only daughter and was in her thirties at the time. While the couple wanted to leave her all their assets after death, they were afraid she would lose her government-provided benefits if those assets ended up in her name. They weren't rich—they only had a couple hundred thousand dollars to leave behind. But they knew that if their daughter lost government assistance, she would be penniless in a short period of time due to her medical expenses and inability to provide for herself. A special needs trust would allow them to leave assets behind that could be doled out over time, allowing her to receive some financial benefit and still maintain her government assistance. In addition, it could minimize her access to the funds, allaying their concerns about her possibly spending the inheritance irresponsibly, commonly known as spendthrift provisions. This trust gave the couple peace of mind in knowing that their daughter, who had depended on them her entire life, would still be taken care of after they were gone.

MEET JOE

Sometimes, the reason for more advanced estate planning is to maximize the legacy of abnormally large estates and avoid unnecessary taxation. I remember Joe, who was single but had a girlfriend he had been with for decades. Joe had more money than he could ever spend, with nearly $10 million in various types of investments. He accumulated so much in part because he was incredibly frugal—he proudly drove the same Chevy Impala to our office for years, saying he had more than 200,000 miles on it. Knowing he wasn't going to be able to spend all his life savings, he recognized a well-defined purpose for most of these funds: maximize their after-tax return for his girlfriend and siblings. With an estate of that size and being a single individual, his estate was staring at a very significant tax upon his passing. Over time, we moved funds into an irrevocable trust that would fund a life insurance policy offering a guaranteed tax-free return on his deposits. Upon death, his current estate would double in size. The trust allowed us to minimize Joe's estate and income taxes while leveraging his insurability. He said it was a great weight lifted off his shoulders—knowing exactly what he was going to leave behind and that it couldn't be squandered due to trust provisions. It would go to exactly who he wanted it to and, ultimately, he would have an impact or legacy. He always said he wanted to be a good steward of his life savings, and putting in place his Purpose-Based Allocation did just that.

If you fall into one of these more complex categories, you will undoubtedly need to meet with an estate planning attorney to discuss your estate planning strategy.

Long-Term Health Care Risks

While most want to avoid any discussion regarding death, even fewer want to address the potential risk of winding up with a long-term health care need during retirement. When most of us think of long-term health care expenses, we often think of gloomy nursing homes with poor staff and unhappy patients.

MEET MY GRANDMOTHER, CHRISTINE

I know this experience well. My grandmother, Christine Weade, required skilled nursing care. Toward the end of her life, she suffered from congestive heart failure and dementia. I was very close to my grandmother growing up, so it was very difficult to see her in this condition. Initially, a stroke landed her in the local hospital. I went to visit her as soon as I could, which wasn't easy in the middle of a blizzard. I walked into her room, hopped into her hospital bed, threw my arm around her and held her close. I was later reprimanded by the nurse for this, and hers weren't the only feathers ruffled by my gesture of familiarity.

My grandfather passed a few years prior, and my grandmother decided to start dating again. As I lay in the hospital bed with my grandmother, her boyfriend walked in. I will never forget the look on his face when he saw me there. We hadn't met before, and this old gentleman quickly turned away and left the room upon seeing a strapping young guy in bed with his lady—a look of disgust on his face. He later confronted my grandmother, wanting to know who that guy was in bed with her. My grandmother was a pretty lively old lady, and she gave him heck even for questioning her.

My grandmother seemed to have trouble remembering who visited her early in the day, so I asked the nurse if she felt it was a sign of Alzheimer's. The nurse told me it was difficult to say at this point, but as time went on, it became clear that she was suffering continual difficulty with her memory. Eventually, after further heart trouble and ongoing memory issues (including not being able to remember to take her medication), she ended up in a skilled nursing care facility.

ESTATE PLANNING

One day, I remember visiting her with my wife, Chelsie. When we came to visit, it said "Welcome, Christine" on her whiteboard in the room. My wife remarked, "That's really sweet of them to welcome you; they must be really nice here." Grandma replied to ask if we could instead cross it out to say, "Goodbye, Christine." She hated it in that nursing home, and I couldn't blame her. It was a sad place to live, and I desperately wanted to get her out. That day, my father called to ask if I was going to visit Grandma sometime soon. I told him we spent a few hours there earlier, but my father had just spoken with her on the phone, and she told him she hadn't seen me in weeks.

A few days later, she enlisted her boyfriend to break her out of the nursing home. He put her in a wheelchair and tried to load her up in his truck for takeoff. It was quite a fiasco, but it gives one an idea of how much she hated it there. Fortunately, she didn't have to be there for long; my spunky grandmother passed away a few weeks after her failed break-out attempt. Given my own grandmother's experience, I understand why people are so reluctant to address the subject of long-term care, but it's important to understand that not all long-term care experiences are negative.

MEET BRIAN AND SHEILA

I once worked with one of the most adorable couples I have ever come across. Sheila was always right by Brian's side, holding his arm or walking hand in hand as they entered the office. You could tell how much they adored one another. She was interested in cars and loved her '69 Camaro—it was always a topic of conversation when we were together. She almost loved it as much as the jewelry her husband gifted to her just to see her smile. They retired a year before we first met and implemented their Retire With Purpose™ Framework. Five years later, she began to forget things. At first, they were the simplest things: where she put the keys or how long she left the lasagna in the oven. The casual observer wouldn't have known it—she seemed as sharp as ever whenever we got together to review their plan.

That soon changed, though. One day, she didn't join us for our review. I immediately asked about it. Sheila never missed an opportunity to spread her hugs and kisses around our office. Brian shared that her condition was getting worse and the doctors had diagnosed her with early-onset Alzheimer's. I couldn't believe it; she was always the sharpest of the two, but now she could no longer remember who I was or where she was. The doctors told Brian she needed to be under 24-hour care; she couldn't be left alone. At one point, he would take Sheila to adult daycare a few times a week, which she thought was great. It was the happiest time of her day, as she assumed she was back in school again. As time went on, Brian's health and ability to care for her waned. He could no longer provide the level of care she needed. It broke his heart, but Sheila had to move to an assisted living facility.

I was so sad for him at first, but the day after he moved her in, he had a smile on his face. He said, "She's happier than I've seen her in months. She's surrounded by friends and even people she knows. There's always something to do, and I just couldn't provide her with that." Sheila loved to dance and socialize, and there was always something going on. Her favorite thing was that the facility gave residents the opportunity to take dance lessons—one of her favorite things to do with Brian.

This allowed Brian to get some of his own life back, as well. He hadn't been able to visit their children and grandchildren for years since Sheila could not travel. Now, he planned trips to see them on a regular basis. He was even able to restore his golf game a bit and go on the occasional fishing trip. Of course, Brian never left Sheila for long. If he wasn't traveling, he was by her side, just trying to make her smile. All of this

ESTATE PLANNING

wouldn't have been possible without the long-term care strategies we put in place as they stepped into retirement. Thankfully, they are both happy and able to continue enjoying the time they have left together years into the future.

The odds of needing long-term health care at some point during retirement for those over the age of sixty-five is around 70 percent.[45] Those odds sound high because they are. If it's hard to believe, maybe it's important for us to define just exactly what long-term health care really is. Long-term health care isn't just nursing home care. It includes a continuum of medical and social services designed to support the needs of people living with chronic health problems that affect their ability to perform everyday activities. These services include three levels of care: in-home, assisted and skilled nursing health care needs. There are different odds of needing each level of care, as well. While the odds of requiring some form of long-term health care are around 70 percent, skilled nursing home care is one of the most likely insurance claims you will probably face during retirement, not to mention the most expensive. The length of the average stay in a skilled nursing care facility is around two and one-half years.[46] The average annual cost is $108,405 nationally for a private room, according to Genworth's 2021 Cost of Care Survey. That's around $271,013 for the average stay with about a fifty-fifty shot of occurrence.[47]

I think it's safe to say we should be having a discussion regarding needs and options at the onset of any truly comprehensive retirement plan—especially if you might face a risk that's about as likely as a financial emergency, market crash, or inflation during your retirement.

Once we face reality, we must ask, what are our payment options? While Medicare may cover your expenses for a short period of time (up to one hundred days of care in some instances), beyond that, you are on your own. That means any payments come directly out of your pocket until you qualify for Medicaid. Qualification for Medicaid varies state by state, but regardless, to qualify, you must spend your own assets first. Medicaid is for those who are financially impoverished, and qualifying for it takes many decisions out of your hands when it comes to the facility and level of care you receive. For instance, home health care, which most families would prefer, is typically out of the question.

Outside of those options, which don't sound all that appealing, we must evaluate some form of long-term care insurance. Despite what you may think, there are many different ways to get long-term care coverage. Some policies come with a traditional insurance premium, while others are asset-based in nature and may or may not require medical qualification. Let's cover some of these major forms of coverage and their pros and cons next.

Traditional Long-Term Care Insurance

Traditional long-term care insurance is like most other insurance coverages that you are used to paying, such as your health, property and casualty insurance. You will pay an annual premium for a specified level of benefits, and it's typically use it or lose it. Insurance companies greatly underestimated the demand that would be placed upon their reserves when these products initially launched. As a result, premiums increased dramatically for these insureds, and many insurance companies either exited the long-term care insurance business or were put out of business altogether.

This understandably created a tremendous amount of negative news coverage. Premiums have reached unaffordable levels for most consumers, and, as such, traditional long-term care insurance policies are rarely used to fund long-term care needs in comparison to its heyday. Rates and benefits are always evolving, so this should still be evaluated as a potential long-term care solution. It's important not to dismiss any option out of hand without kicking the tires first, so to speak. In addition, some employers may offer discounted long-term care solutions at a much more affordable price. For instance, I had a client who was evaluating long-term care insurance policies and I recommended we first check with his human resources department to see if his employer offered a viable solution. Luckily, he had access to a policy that would only cost $600 per year for $250,000 in benefits—adjusted annually for inflation. A similar product with a private insurer could cost thousands of dollars per year for equivalent benefits.

Asset-Based Life Insurance Solutions

The gentleman in the preceding example was married, and his wife unfortunately didn't have the same kind of employer-subsidized policy available. For her, we decided to explore an asset-based solution. They had an overflow emergency fund of $100,000 sitting at the bank. From that, they moved $75,000 to a product that would earn minimal interest, slightly better than the bank. They could get their money back at any time, and if they had a long-term care need, this product would provide similar benefits to the husband's employer-based plan. This would not require any ongoing premiums, but instead, it would just require a rearranging of assets. They never planned on using that emergency fund, but it was there if they needed it. One of the ironic things is that the circumstance for which they would most likely have used their emergency fund was a long-term health care event. Now, it was still available for any number of reasons, but they had extra benefits for long-term care needs. Additionally, if they never used the money, the long-term care benefits would pass on as a tax-free death benefit to their heirs.

As I mentioned before, it's about finding the closest distance between two points—a straight line—to maximize the efficiency of the dollars you have saved for retirement. This couple's emergency money was arranged most efficiently for their purpose—adding value without adding cost. On the other hand, if they were willing to give up control of the funds entirely, we could have provided even greater benefits. In this instance, however, they would have lost their overflow emergency fund due to penalties and/or costs that could eat into the cash deposit.

MEET MICHAEL AND SUSAN

In some instances, riders can be attached to these asset-based plans, providing extended benefits for a minimal annual premium. For example, Michael and Susan had an IRA they did not need for retirement income. We already satisfied the first three areas of their L.I.F.E. Plan and were left with additional IRA funds, which they knew they would be forced to take RMDs from—RMDs they did not need. These additional required distributions would cause frustrating taxation. Still, that could all be smoothed out if they began taking distributions now rather than later when the account was larger (a larger balance would require larger taxable distributions).

Michael and Susan decided to take small annual distributions from the account over a period of ten years and move the funds into an asset-based, long-term care policy, satisfying both of their long-term care needs. In addition, we attached a rider that they would need to pay for separately out of their monthly cash flow but would allow for benefits to continue as long as they needed care—even after the benefit pool was used up. This not only filled their most likely needs but provided additional reassurance. Regardless of how long they needed the care, they would have coverage. It also allowed for a tax-free death benefit to pass onto the heirs should they be lucky enough not to need long-term care.

Traditional Life Insurance Policies with Accelerated Death Benefit Provisions

Life insurance solutions have evolved tremendously over the years, providing more benefits at a lower and more predictable cost than in years past. Many permanent policies also include provisions that allow you to have "living benefits." These provide you with the ability to spend down your death benefit even while you are alive for qualifying events, such as long-term care or disability needs. This is the solution I have chosen for myself and my father's long-term care solutions.

For myself, I needed to have traditional life insurance to protect my family's financial well-being in case of my death. When I purchased my life insurance policies, I used policies that have provisions to accelerate paying out a death benefit while I'm living in case of critical, chronic and/or terminal illness. These policies also double as a disability benefit solution in case I become disabled. When I evaluated traditional long-term disability insurance, it seemed extremely expensive. In addition, I knew I could potentially be throwing thousands of dollars down the drain should I never use the policy benefits, which is how most retirees feel about traditional long-term care insurance. As such, I could pay for term insurance to cover temporary needs, including debt and expenses, at a younger age. At the same time, I could use cash-value-based life insurance policies as a source of tax-free retirement income if I didn't need to use the death benefit prior for disability and/or health care expenses.

In the case of my father, he was divorced when we picked out his coverage. That was important because we wanted to identify the reason for the coverage in the first place. In many cases, long-term care coverage is picked up not just to protect the estate but to ensure the healthy spouse is not left destitute with major long-term health care expenses for the spouse who needs care. In my dad's case, he had plenty of assets to self-insure or pay for those expenses out of pocket; in other words, I was the one who would be left essentially footing the bill with my inheritance.

My father built a beautiful home in Asheville, North Carolina, that he absolutely loved. One day, I remember him sending me pictures of the sun rising over the mountains, followed by a phone call in which he said, "Someday, son, this will be yours." I said, "You're right, as long as we don't have to sell it to pay for the nursing home," laughing, of course. He offered a flippant response, saying the only way that would ever happen was if he couldn't find the gun. Of course, he recognized that if he needed nursing home care, he probably wouldn't be able to find the gun in the first place. I decided to purchase a $500,000 life insurance policy on him. There was no reason for him to purchase the policy himself since he had assets he could use to pay for potential care. I purchased it as an investment in my inheritance and as a guaranteed tax-free return for my annual savings. It would accelerate the death benefit in case he needed long-term care coverage and would ultimately pay out a tax-free death benefit on his passing in case he never experienced a long-term care need.

In many instances, I run into clients who have old, active life insurance policies they plan to pass to their children someday, many with substantial cash values they don't need for retirement. These cash values will be left to the insurance company, ultimately, with the life insurance company itself only needing to pay out the difference between the cash value in the policy and the death benefit. Let me map this out. I met with a couple whose life insurance policy contained cash value that would allow for the death benefit to stay in force for the rest of their lives without any further premiums. We exchanged the old policy for a new one while maintaining the same cash values and death benefit. Now, though, the new policy would also allow them to utilize the death benefit in case of a long-term care need. It didn't cost them anything to make the exchange, but they picked up benefits they would not have had otherwise.

After stress-testing their overall plan following this simple move, we found a small gap in long-term care needs that could be filled with a low-cost, low-benefit traditional long-term care insurance policy. In other instances, we may choose to give up the cash value in the policy for a bigger death and long-term care benefit. This is because you may never plan to use the cash value for your own purposes anyway. If you let the cash value ride idle without utilizing it to purchase a bigger death benefit, then the insurance carrier must only pay out the difference between the cash value and the specified death benefit. That means you foot the bill for the rest. Get that cash value to work, and don't let them just slide it in their pocket when you've left this mortal plane.

Asset-Based Annuities with Long-Term Care Riders

One of the biggest downsides to traditional long-term care insurance, or even life insurance with accelerated death benefit provisions, is the requirement that the insured pass a health exam. Many people seeking long-term care coverage of some kind may be of an age or health history that makes qualifying for this insurance unlikely or unaffordable. In this case, you may want to evaluate annuities with long-term care riders that do not require you to pass a medical exam and are not necessarily age-dependent.

MEET RICHARD AND LUCY

Richard and Lucy were very serious about long-term care concerns. They watched Lucy's mother deplete all her retirement assets to pay for nursing home care. Sadly, Richard's multiple bouts with cancer made him nearly uninsurable via long-term care insurance or traditional life insurance policies. The few policies they qualified for were prohibitively expensive due to their age. Instead, they turned to annuities that had guaranteed lifetime withdrawal benefit (GLWB) riders with long-term care provisions. The guaranteed income benefits would satisfy Richard and Lucy's retirement income needs for the rest of their lives. If either of them needed long-term health care, the guaranteed income benefits they were using to meet their monthly spending needs would double for a period of five years. After that, the income would drop back to their original guaranteed income benefit for the remainder of their lives. This satisfied the most likely level of care they would encounter should they need it. The annuity Richard and Lucy purchased would pay out following a long-term care need that persisted beyond ninety days if a physician verified they could not perform two out of six activities of daily living (ADLs). It would also cover all three levels of care: home health care, assisted living and skilled nursing care. The benefits of these contracts will vary, so be sure you pay attention to elimination periods and the type of coverage that will qualify for benefit payout.

> For more on this topic, check out our YouTube channel and watch our video, "Traditional vs. Hybrid Long-Term Care. Which Is Right For Me?":
>
> HOWARDBAILEY.COM/LTC

Legacy Maximization

So far, we have discussed how you can implement a basic estate plan, ensure your assets will pass to your loved ones as efficiently as possible, and preserve those assets from major long-term care expenses. Now, we must turn our attention to ensuring Uncle Sam is cut out of the picture. The last thing you need is to make Uncle Sam the biggest beneficiary of your life savings. He may need the financial assistance, but you should never leave too much to someone who's that fiscally irresponsible.

Basic IRA Strategies

One of the biggest liabilities most retirees will face is the tax-deferred benefit accounts they have accrued over their lifetimes. This mainly consists of individual retirement accounts (IRAs) and 401(k)s, in addition to other employer-sponsored retirement plans. These assets are not only taxable upon distribution to yourself but also to your heirs upon death. Some of the most basic planning starts with determining how to best distribute these tax-deferred accounts upon your death.

Stretch IRA

Some of the biggest liabilities most retirees will face are the tax-deferred accounts they have accrued over their lifetimes. These mainly consist of individual retirement accounts (IRAs) and 401(k)s, in addition to other employer-sponsored retirement plans. These assets are not only taxable upon distribution to yourself but also to your heirs upon death. Some of the most basic planning starts with determining how to best distribute these tax-deferred accounts upon your death.

IRAs, often retirees' largest assets, can be troublesome for survivors because of their precarious tax situation. As deferred assets, IRAs have never been taxed, and Uncle Sam is determined to get his portion. For a surviving spouse, inheriting an IRA is as easy as replacing the original owner's name with your own or even rolling those assets into your existing IRA.

Until recently, it was possible to designate a child or grandchild as beneficiary and take minimum distributions based on their life expectancy over the course of their lives—a technique known as a "Stretch IRA"—effectively preserving the tax-advantaged nature of the account for an additional generation or more; however, the passing of the SECURE Act in 2019 eliminated this option for non-spouse beneficiaries.[48] Now, these beneficiaries are required to distribute the full amount of the inherited IRA within ten years of death. This further reinforces the need for tax planning for your estate.

Take, for instance, a sixty-year-old couple with a million-dollar traditional IRA growing at 7.2 percent per year. Without consideration of any required minimum distributions, the value of that IRA would double twice by the time they reached the age of eighty, bringing it to $4 million dollars. Assuming no growth in the value of the IRA over the ten-year distribution period, there would be an annual distribution

ESTATE PLANNING

of approximately $400,000 per year. Assuming a 30 percent effective tax rate, the total taxes paid over the ten-year period would be $1.2 million, more than the value of their IRA at sixty. It could be enraging to imagine that the current value of your IRA could go entirely into Uncle Sam's pocket without implementing a strategy to avoid it. Enter the value of the Roth conversion.

Roth Conversion

You may be saying, "Wait a minute, Casey, I thought Roth IRAs didn't have RMDs." You're right. During the lifetime of the owner, Roth IRAs don't have RMDs. Yet, after the original account owner has passed, the beneficiaries must withdraw the full value of the account over ten years in accordance with the SECURE Act and SECURE Act 2.0. However, unlike traditional IRA distributions, Roth IRA distributions are still income-tax-free. If you recall in a previous chapter, we discussed converting as much of your traditional IRA into a Roth IRA as possible before RMDs kick in. When it comes to legacy planning, another question to ask is: even after you are seventy-three and have begun taking RMDs, are you still in a lower income tax bracket than your likely heirs? If so, it might still be worth converting your traditional IRA—even at a higher tax bracket for you—into a Roth account, saving taxes for your beneficiaries down the road.

Here's another way to think about it. Think of a home loan. When you take out a long-term mortgage, you know the interest rate that will be paid and the cumulative amount of interest to be paid over the life of the loan. If you are like me, you would never take out a long-term loan with a variable interest rate without a cap on the maximum rate that could be charged. However, with a tax-deductible retirement account, that is exactly what you have done. You have borrowed money in the form of a tax deduction without knowing the tax rate you or your heirs will be charged at some point in the future. If your goal is to retire debt-free, don't forget about your loan from the IRS in the form of tax deferral. It could be the most expensive loan you have ever taken.

Distribution Strategies

In addition to stretching your IRAs upon death and converting them to Roth IRAs, you may want to consider ways of creating a more substantial tax-free death benefit for your heirs through the use of a life insurance strategy.

My dad is currently doing this with his nonqualified, tax-deferred annuities, but the strategy can also apply to systematic distributions for tax-deferred retirement plans. In my family, legacy has been very important, starting with my grandfather leaving my father a modest sum of money. My dad has the goal of passing this inheritance down and adding to it for the next generation, and I also have a similar goal. He knows that during retirement, he will likely be in a lower tax bracket than I will be when I ultimately inherit those tax-deferred assets. So, as he distributes those tax-deferred assets over time, he is re-depositing them into tax-free life insurance policies that will offer a guaranteed, tax-free rate of return to his beneficiaries. They will also immediately offer substantially more benefits than would ever be seen from the tax-deferred annuities he is using to pay for the policies. In his case, he is only insuring himself, but in other cases, we are working with couples who want to maximize their legacy for their next generation together.

Leveraging the lives of two individuals allows us substantially more in benefits than just one individual through survivorship (a.k.a. second-to-die) life insurance strategies. These types of policies will not pay out until the death of both individuals. As such, the insurance company can get more predictability regarding life expectancy, offering more

ESTATE PLANNING

leverage for larger death benefits. One couple I worked with had goals of maximizing the legacy they would leave behind, as we more than satisfied their other needs in the first three areas of their L.I.F.E. Plan.

We used portions of their RMDs to purchase traditional life insurance with accelerated death benefit provisions as their long-term care solution. We also used excess assets to fund a survivorship life insurance policy offering four times the death benefits that could be achieved when insuring only a single life. The neat thing about their survivorship policy is that it also came with an accelerated death benefit provision for long-term health care needs. The accelerated benefits could only be paid out after the death of the first insured, which was in line with their wishes. They expect the first person to need long-term care will have substantial assistance from their spouse. After one spouse dies, the remaining person may be at higher risk of needing institutional care because they will not have a spouse to rely on. The most liberating part of this strategy was that they recreated the entire current size of their estate with the survivorship life insurance policy. They knew that if they spent all their other assets, they would still leave behind the same amount of assets they had on day one of the plan through the survivorship policy death benefit.

This couple previously felt apprehensive about spending their money. They wanted to ensure they did not spend the principal they hoped to leave to their heirs. Now, they could spend with the confidence of knowing that if they spent everything else (which would still be unlikely), they would preserve the current assets they had at the onset of the strategy. This strategy can be very advantageous to couples at odds over what they want to leave behind for the next generation. Many times, couples have different ideas of what the purpose of their life savings really is. While one may feel no responsibility to leave behind a legacy for the next generation, the other may feel very strongly about financially benefiting those they leave behind. I will often sit with couples in our first strategy visits and hear them discover just how different their goals are.

MEET DON AND LORI

Once, I worked with a lovely couple, Don and Lori, with whom I walked through our Retire With Purpose™ Framework. They did a great job of saving for retirement. They weren't big earners, but they were tremendous savers. We filled each of their first three L.I.F.E. buckets and still had funds left over to put toward a substantial legacy. I sensed some angst coming from Lori's side of the table and asked how she felt about our direction. She said she didn't understand why they worked their whole lives, pinched their pennies and sacrificed just so they could leave it all behind, and then some—to their children. Lori felt that they had done enough already since she and Don had raised their kids, put them through school and helped them buy their first home. Don, though, felt it was an obligation they owed to the next generation.

As we dug deeper, it became apparent that Don harbored some resentments from his own experiences. You see, his parents spent their life savings and, later in life, not only did they have nothing monetarily to leave behind, but their circumstances forced their children—including Don—to shoulder many of their financial burdens. In a certain sense, Don wanted to make up for his parents' shortcomings—something Lori hadn't realized was still burdening him. Using our Retire With Purpose™ Framework, though, Don and Lori found a compromise that allowed them to have their cake and eat it, too.

ESTATE PLANNING

Inheritances: IRA and 401(k)

A final word on IRA and 401(k) inheritances: if you have RMDs you don't need, in addition to triggering taxes on Social Security and increasing your Medicare premiums, you may also consider the ongoing tax implications of where you put those dollars once they come out of your IRA. If you have no need for the dollars and ultimately expect to pass them on to your heirs, it might make more sense to reallocate them to life insurance policies on which you and your heirs will not be taxed. If you may need the funds in the future and you or your spouse are still working, you may be able to reallocate a portion or all of those distributions as a Roth IRA contribution up to the maximum contribution limit; otherwise, these funds should be invested in an after-tax portfolio focused on minimizing on-going taxation through tax-efficient investment strategies.

4 TAX BUCKETS

Taxable	Tax-Deferred	Income Tax Free	Income & Estate Tax Free
Bank Brokerage Trust	401(k) IRA Nonqualified Annuity Savings Bond	Municipal Bonds Roth IRA Roth 401(k) Life Insurance	Irrevocable Life Insurance Trust Charitable Remainder Trust Special Trusts

Annuity Legacy Strategies

If you still aspire to maximize the guaranteed legacy for your heirs but don't qualify for some of the previously discussed life insurance strategies due to age or health, it may behoove you to evaluate annuity death benefit strategies that don't require health exams or ongoing premiums.

Along these lines, I once had a retiree who had no goals of spending down her IRA and had no need for the annual RMDs. In addition, she was in her early seventies and had a heart condition that made her unlikely to qualify for life insurance. Instead, we used an annuity contract that guaranteed her account would continue to grow in terms of death benefits, even as she satisfied the minimum distribution requirements. She had peace of mind that her RMDs would never eat into her principal.

In another case, we met with a gentleman in his late seventies who was not in the best of health. As a result, we were able to allocate his funds to an account with a substantial upfront bonus. He passed away two years later, but the principal and bonus enabled additional dollars to pass to the next generation—more so than going the route of taking on substantial market risk over the same period.

Annuity death benefits come in many forms: sometimes as upfront bonuses, guaranteed growth rates, daily step-ups in value due to market returns and even multiples of market returns. The downside is that annuities do not pass tax-free to your heirs unless they are held inside a Roth IRA. As such, life insurance is typically the more attractive option. The correct option for you and your family will be dependent on factors that include your age, tax qualification of the account, your health, risk tolerance and general financial situation.

ESTATE PLANNING

TAKEAWAYS, ACTIONS AND NOTES

What are your biggest takeaways from this chapter?

_____
_____
_____
_____
_____
_____
_____

What are three action steps that you should work on now?

1. _____
2. _____
3. _____

What are three action steps for later?

1. _____
2. _____
3. _____

JOB OPTIONAL

NOTES:

CHAPTER SEVEN

CLOSING

When to start: Ahh—the age-old question of when to begin planning for retirement. It bewilders me that this is even a question. When should you begin saving, paying off your debt or setting yourself up for a career, for that matter? We're talking about your future here. We should be planning for this in some form or another from the moment we are conscious that it is a need. Why wait for something that is inevitably going to come if we live long enough (which we all hope to) in the first place? We must always be planning with a purpose.

Money without a purpose is just a dollar sign, and accumulating wealth should always have a more powerful purpose behind it, or you will be left unfulfilled.

Of course, there are different things to focus on at different stages of your financial life, but all should have the goal of creating financial security, and not just for the short term.

Let's start by looking at each stage, what your focus should be and what type of financial professional you should be working with, if any. I've seen some financial life cycle breakdowns that involved as many as ten or more phases of financial life. However, there are really two areas of focus for most financial professionals: the accumulation phase and the spend-down phase of retirement.

COMPETING PRIORITIES

	Accumulation Advisor	Retirement Advisor
First Priority	Growth	Income
Second Priority	Safety	Safety
Third Priority	Income	Growth

While most financial professionals have the same priorities, the order of those priorities differs based on what kind of advisor they are.

Accumulation

In the accumulation stage, you may be just starting out, or perhaps you are well into your career. The good thing is that you have time on your side before you need the funds you are saving. Your focus will most likely begin with paying down debt and transitioning into saving as much as possible out of every paycheck while still living comfortably. This is the stage at which very few individuals really need a financial advisor in the first place. Your goal is to accumulate as much as possible so you may reach financial independence as soon as possible. Here, you want to maximize growth efficiency. Of course, this starts with finding those areas that work against your growth—draining your return potential. Most likely, this is due to debt, such as credit card and student loan debt. After you attack those areas of your financial life, it's time to begin investing.

You may think it's time to run out and find a financial advisor to get you started. The reality is that most people don't need a financial advisor to help them establish retirement savings accounts and invest. In this technology age, you can hop online and find a low-cost brokerage to open an IRA or Roth IRA; that is, if your employer doesn't offer a retirement plan and you start making systematic contributions (taking advantage of that dollar-cost averaging principle stipulated earlier in the book). Statistically, most financial advisors, brokers and even the best money managers likely won't beat the index they use as their benchmark. [49]

They also usually won't beat the broader stock market as a whole. It may take a little reading, but if you are comfortable picking your own holdings or sticking with broader stock market index funds, you will keep costs low. In addition, it is probable you will beat most advisors out there to whom you would otherwise pay 1 or 2 percent per year.

If you're not comfortable building a portfolio yourself, there are plenty of robotic advisory firms that charge substantially less than the advisor down the street. They help pick the initial funds, rebalance regularly and even conduct automatic tax harvesting, if necessary. Your primary goal is to keep your cost of investing low; that includes ongoing taxation, as well.

If you are in the minority of younger individuals with substantial incomes or are a business owner with tax planning concerns, then maybe it might be time to hire a financial advisor and justify the cost. The reality is that a financial advisor doesn't typically need to be hired until you require protection against major financial liabilities you are facing. When you are younger, this is most likely death, disability and taxation.

At Howard Bailey, we also have some younger clients who are ten-plus years out from retirement without a need for extensive financial planning.

The Red Zone

When you get within five to ten years from retirement, you reach what is often referred to as "the Red Zone." You find yourself at a point in life where the mistakes made over the coming years could make or break your retirement. As retirement specialists, most families we work with are ready to begin structuring their retirement strategy or are already in retirement and prepared to implement a real plan for their future. The sooner you take the initiative to sit with an advisor and begin planning, the greater the chance you will have to retire as planned. You may feel you have plenty of time to continue to take on the risks you have in the past, but the reality may be to the contrary.

MEET NATE AND ERICA

As an example, Nate and Erica visited with us five years away from retirement. They invested their entire retirement savings in their 401(k), and their investing position had been about the same for the last twenty-plus years. We recommended that they begin reallocating their 401(k) to reduce their overall risk level. They had a substantial amount of their 401(k) funds invested into an employer stock fund. Nate felt the company was doing well, and they always made up losses in past market crashes over a five-year period. We shared analyses with him that illustrated it wasn't just making up losses that would be necessary over the following five-year period. They would need to see a modest annual growth rate as well, or they would not be able to retire as planned. Nate and Erica followed our advice and reallocated their 401(k) with their first five years of income needs positioned in a fixed income portfolio at minimal risk. Over the following twelve months, the employer stock lost nearly half its value due to organizational changes that were unforeseen by any of the employees. During their next review, Nate and Erica mentioned that many of their co-workers would not be able to retire as planned and would have to continue to work for many more years. They, on the other hand, would be able to retire as planned due to their diversified allocations. Not only that but over the coming years, they enjoyed their work more than they did at any time before. They no longer had the stress of worrying about whether retirement would work out or not and whether they were saving enough. Erica said it gave them great peace of mind knowing they could step away from work at any time as they were now in "Job Optional" status.

MEET TOM AND JENI

On another note, it pays to get a jump-start on your health care planning as well. This fact was illustrated to me directly after implementing our Retire With Purpose™ Framework for a couple in their fifties. When we first laid out Tom and Jeni's strategy, they heard their sixties were the best time to examine long-term health care solutions. At the meeting, they immediately questioned why we would implement a long-term care strategy before they reached that necessary age but took the advice anyway. Not even two months after putting their long-term health care strategy in force, Jeni was diagnosed with an aggressive form of cancer. While she would likely overcome the disease, she was unqualified for any life or long-term care insurance policy moving forward. Luckily, we had already put their long-term care strategy in motion, so the diagnosis couldn't erase her chances at coverage.

Sometimes, retirement preparedness is more about organizing expenses and debt than anything else. When it comes to a successful retirement, you often hear it's all about a successful retirement income strategy. This is true, but that starts with identifying expenses. We visited with a couple who were several years from retirement, yet they didn't think they would ever retire due to their expenses compared to their savings. They had substantial credit card and mortgage debt that was sopping up large portions of their monthly budget. On a thorough review, we reorganized their debt so they would pay it off by the time they wished to retire. We also freed up additional cash to put away for retirement. Now, they will retire on time with a new outlook on life in their golden years.

It's never too late to begin your retirement planning, and I would wrap estate planning into that strategy, as well. While I see many who are tempted to designate estate planning as a separate stage in their financial life, in my experience, this segmentation results in putting off decisions for scenarios that could occur much sooner than expected. We had a couple in their eighties who came to us under the assumption that it was too late for them to do anything. They wanted to have a second look, nonetheless. Together, they had roughly $3 million in various investment accounts, over $2 million of which was invested in taxable mutual funds. Their frustration was mostly with their annual tax bill. They were being taxed on mutual fund distributions they weren't spending in addition to substantial required minimum distributions. I often state this as "spending money on money you're not spending." They were paying more taxes than they ever had throughout their lifetime. We managed to shelter those funds from ongoing taxation and structure a strategy to pass them on to their heirs tax-free as well. In addition,

CLOSING

they were able to take advantage of qualified charitable distributions (QCDs) to satisfy charitable goals and eliminate their RMDs from their tax return.[50] In the end, these relatively simple changes will most likely put tens, if not hundreds, of thousands of dollars back in their pockets over the remaining years of their lives—all after they thought nothing could be done. The moral of the story: While it's never too early to plan for a comprehensive retirement plan, it's never too late, either!

A Written Plan

Let me share with you a quick story. Maybe you've heard it before, but it's one of my favorites. Dr. Albert Einstein was traveling from New York to Chicago in the late 1920s—by train, of course. Einstein boarded the train, and the conductor began passing through the cabin, collecting and punching tickets. As he approached Einstein, he noticed a concerned look on his face while shuffling through his pockets. The conductor recognized the famous doctor and told him not to worry about the ticket, as he knew he was good for it. While the conductor passed back through the cabin, he noticed Einstein still looking very disheveled, even more so than the last time he walked by. As Einstein stood on his chair looking through the luggage racks, the conductor said, "Dr. Einstein, please have a seat; we know who you are. Your ticket is really unnecessary." The concerned doctor replied, "Sir, I know who I am; the problem is I don't know where I am going!"

Based on the thousands of pre-retirees and retirees I engage with each year, I estimate that fewer than 20 percent of retirees have a written plan for retirement. That written plan is your ticket for a successful retirement—your ticket to avoid the level of concern the conductor saw on Dr. Einstein's face.

When you ultimately structure a retirement strategy, it should be put in writing so you know not only what your destination is but also how you will get there. A retirement plan is not a stack of statements. It's not a simulation stating you have a percentage chance of success, and it's certainly not an investment strategy. A retirement plan is documentation for how each of your assets will specifically assist you in retirement as well as how that strategy will deliver more meaning and purpose to your life. Moreover, it lays out the main risks you will face during retirement and how you will overcome them as they occur. Where will you turn in case of emergency? Where will your income come from in case of a market downturn? Where will you generate additional income in case of inflation? How will you cover potential long-term care expenses? How will you manage ongoing taxation in addition to avoiding taxes as you leave those assets behind to the next generation?

Choosing the Right Financial Planner

I want to offer a few important points to keep in mind when you are trying to find the right financial advisor for you and your family. We're not always the right fit for the people who come into our office, and they aren't always the right fit for us. This must be a mutual decision on behalf of both parties since you could be starting a lifelong relationship—that is, unless your advisor is nearing retirement age themselves. Let's start there.

Age and Business Continuity

One consideration when you seek a financial advisor is the age of that person. You should strongly consider whether the advisor (or a capable replacement within that firm) will be around when you're retired and when they are supposed to be managing YOUR retirement. You don't want to be left looking for a new advisor when you're eighty-five years old.

Our team once saw a wave of new clients come to us from another advisory firm run by a gentleman who decided to up and retire one day. Most of these clients said their advisor was older than they were when they started working with him, yet they didn't think anything of it. One woman in particular, Shirley, explained that she didn't hire the advisor in the first place. Her husband did. She lost her husband a few years prior to the retirement of their advisor, and she didn't know where to begin looking for a replacement. Shirley interviewed three other advisors before hiring our firm, and she said a key determinant for that was the average age of our team. This was in addition to knowing there was always someone prepared and ready, even if her primary advisor decided to retire. There is no question that experience is one of the most important aspects of finding the right advisor, but there should be no lack of emphasis placed on longevity as well.

Independence

It is incredibly important to find a financial advisor who is independent, not an employee of a large firm. There are many firms at which brokers and advisors can work. I started in the business as an employee of a large brokerage firm. Employees there were told what products and funds to recommend. We were told that what we had to offer was perfect for everyone.

I soon came to realize this was the wrong approach, but unfortunately, this still occurs today. During those days, I often used a tool I was told to sell and would soon find that a tool my dad used as an independent financial advisor was less expensive and had more benefits!

You may be apprehensive about working with an independent advisor. While you don't have the feeling of security a big box name brand firm offers, you don't need to be concerned if you understand what to look out for. Every independent advisor should have what is known as a third-party custodian.

A third-party custodian can ensure advisors don't take your money and run. A third-party custodian acts as an intermediary between the advisory firm and the client. Under this approach, your advisor will never handle client checks, deposits or withdrawals directly. In nearly every theft by an advisor from client funds, there was no third-party custodian involved.

In many instances, the client wrote checks made out in the financial advisor's name or in that of their firm. To sum it up, a third-party custodian acts as the policeman—ensuring your funds stay in your name at all times. Some examples of the largest third-party custodians include Fidelity, Charles Schwab, Pershing and TD Ameritrade. You can also be assured you are always receiving a statement from these third parties and not directly from your advisor—where there is room for fabrication. In the end, the same degree of safety and security can be afforded for your life savings with an independent advisor, along with all the other benefits that come along with it.

Chemistry

Another prime consideration is "chemistry." It's very important that you feel the person you are talking to understands you. If you are a husband and wife, make sure the person talks to both of you. Make sure the advisor also listens to both of you. If you feel for one moment that a broker is dismissing you or your feelings, insulting you or coming across as arrogant, this is the wrong person to work with.

You need to choose an advisor who understands you, listens to you and will put together a financial plan that fits your needs and goals. Remember, it's your money, not theirs!

Empathy

Does the advisor understand you and feel like you do when it comes to your important issues? You may have a special-needs child who requires special planning. You may come from a very poor family—one who lived through the Great Depression. You're worried about running out of money. Can that advisor relate? It's critical that the advisor listens and feels empathy for your particular fears. Another clue you're working with the wrong advisor is if they do not understand or, worse, do not listen.

Community Recognition

The broker or advisor you choose should have a recognized name in the community. Let's think about a company like Google. In Palo Alto, if somebody even writes the word "Google" on a sign, Google comes after them to take that word down. Why? Google ensures it has the legal right to force the issue. For what reason? They will do it simply because they want to protect their reputation, which they feel is second to none.

Other companies that have a very high level of brand recognition, such as McDonald's and Pepsi, will do almost anything to protect that brand.

Conscientious firms may decide not to take certain customers because they worry those customers might be the complaining type. The companies want to protect both their reputation and brand. The same goes for financial advisors. Financial advisors who have a recognized name in a community will be very careful to bend over backward to do the right thing. Why? Because they spent years building their strong reputations, and they don't want anything to tarnish them. Choose an advisor who has a well-recognized name in the community.

Education

Not much is required to hang out one's shingle as a financial advisor. The unfortunate truth is that many financial advisors lack the education, knowledge, credentials and experience required to carry you through the ups and downs of your golden years. The bar for entry into the financial profession is set quite low. Many firms do not even require a college degree. Many states, in fact, require no formal education. In contrast, however, some advisors put themselves through grueling, rigorous, and extensive educational programs to obtain such designations as CERTIFIED FINANCIAL PLANNER™ professional and chartered financial analyst (CFA®). So, asking for an advisor's education and experience is fundamental in your search. I believe it should be one of the first questions you ask.

In addition, there are literally hundreds of designations and certifications that are deceptively impressive. Many advisors hold impressive-sounding credentials, some of which represent impressive achievements, but most do not. Before selecting your advisor, make sure you understand

CLOSING

what their credentials really represent. For instance, a CERTIFIED FINANCIAL PLANNER™ professional must have:

- Graduated with a bachelor's degree (or higher) from an accredited college or university
- Successfully completed college or university-levelcoursework encompassing the areas of financial planning, insurance planning, investment planning, income tax planning, retirement planning, estate planning and interpersonal communication
- Completed the CFP® Board's Financial Plan Development Course, requiring the presentation of a financial plan to the CFP® Board
- Completed a rigorous pass/fail exam administered at a secure facility
- Must have 6,000 hours of personal financial planning experience or 4,000 hours of apprenticeship experience that meets additional requirements
- Passed the CFP® Board's Fitness Standards for Candidates and Registrants
- Completed thirty hours of continuing education every two years

In sharp contrast, the Certified Retirement Financial Advisor Certification Board only requires a four-day classroom course—no prior work experience and no higher education. However, you are required to complete fifteen hours of continuing education per year, which can often be taken online by simply bypassing the class and taking a quiz. While this designation may sound very similar to a CERTIFIED FINANCIAL PLANNER™, the two are in no way comparable. The financial services industry requires financial advisors to establish credibility with their clients. For this reason, an entire credentialing sector now exists to satisfy industry demand. Believe it or not, you could "earn" all these credentials in fewer than thirty days—no prior work experience required![51]

- CAC – Certified Annuity Consultant – one-day class
- APP – Asset Protection Planner – twelve-hour online or in person
- LTCIS – Long-Term Care Insurance Strategist – two-day class
- AIF – Accredited Investment Fiduciary – two-and-one-half-day class
- CCPS – Certified College Planning Specialist – eighteen to twenty-five hours self-study
- CWPP – Certified Wealth Preservation Planner – twenty-four hours online or in person
- CFG – Certified Financial Gerontologist – twenty-four hours self-study
- CSC – Certified Senior Consultant – twenty-five hours self-study
- CSA – Certified Senior Advisor – three-and-one-half-day "live" class
- AIFA – Accredited Investment Fiduciary Auditor – three-and-one-half-day class
- CDS – Certified Divorce Specialist – four-day workshop
- CRFA – Certified Retirement Financial Advisor – four-day class

Experience

The failure rate for legitimate financial advisors is incredibly high. It is one of the most difficult professions to succeed in—with the long hours and high level of education required. According to Zippia (a career-resources site), over 90 percent of financial advisors do not last three years.[52] That is why I recommend you find an advisor with a minimum of five years in practice. Many financial advisors have a high level of sales experience and are extremely charismatic, but personality can only take you so far.

Compensation

We often think discussing payment is rude. After all, it's a big social faux pas to ask someone how much they get paid. Yet, when someone is performing a service for you—whether it's a doctor talking about surgery or a plumber talking about your bathroom remodel—you wouldn't think twice about asking questions like, "How much will this cost?" or, "Should we pay upfront or wait for a bill?" The same should apply to your financial advisor; it shouldn't be a dark secret how much you pay for the service you receive.

There are three ways a financial advisor might get paid: fee-only, commission-only or fee-based. Each has its own advantages and disadvantages, which I will briefly touch on. Your bottom line here is whether you trust your advisor and whether you believe you get an adequate level of value in return for what you pay.

Fee-only advisors charge clients directly through a consultation fee, an hourly rate, a charge for services or a payment based on the percentage of assets under their management. This helps advisors remain independent, but a tradeoff is that a fee-only advisor might be more aggressive in their approach because the more aggressively your portfolio grows, the more money goes into their pocket. In addition, you may be in charge of implementing the plan, which may not be your forte. Not to mention, there may be limitations on product offerings as very few insurance products are available on a fee-only basis without a commission. This could potentially leave you stuck in the investment world with gaps in your strategy in the way of long-term care, life insurance and/or guaranteed income.

Commission-based advisors get a commission for sales, whether that is a percentage of assets assessed as an upfront fee, a kickback from a company whose product they sold or a surcharge for each stock purchase/sale a client makes. Sometimes, these advisors offer more diverse products than a fee-only advisor, but the downside of this approach is that a commission-based advisor must always be selling, possibly incentivizing them to use products that have high turnover rates. There is also the potential for conflicts of interest in offering a certain product that might have a higher commission than another.

Fee-based advisors do a little of both. They might charge a fee to write up a financial plan for a client. Once the plan is implemented, an ongoing fee related to the management of a securities portfolio may be received, along with commissions related to the placement of insurance products. This gives the financial advisor an incentive to grow a client's at-risk investment portfolio, but since their compensation isn't only based on assets under management, they have more leeway to seek insurance-based risk management strategies. Of course, the potential conflict of interest regarding higher incentive commission products still exists, but you have the potential for a broader range of products available to solve your unique needs.

There is no "perfect" compensation model, yet it is important to understand how your advisor makes money and how much will come from your pocket. You can then make a realistic determination about whether the service you receive is in line with what you pay.

> For more on this topic, check out the Podcast section of the Howard Bailey website and watch our video, "Your Financial Advisor May Not Actually Be An 'Advisor'":
>
> HOWARDBAILEY.COM/133

Your Investment Team

When looking for your retirement advisor, recognize the value of a team approach. In retirement, your financial life becomes much more complicated. You will need to ensure all your bases are covered—mainly those of taxation, estate planning and financial planning. Your retirement advisor should act as the quarterback of this team, assisting you with not only developing and implementing your plan but also bringing a team of experts to the table.

In the world of finance, we all have our areas of expertise. The certified public accountant (CPA) has extensive experience in accounting and tax matters. The attorney who specializes in estate planning will naturally have extensive experience in estate law. Your financial professional should have general knowledge and experience in both, as well as in handling your investments. You will most likely need these experts to work as a team, with your financial advisor acting as a quarterback or general contractor.

I will issue a note of caution, however. Be careful when you're exploring all-in-one firms. By this, I mean firms that boast of having all the professionals you need under one roof. They might have a CPA, an estate planning attorney, a financial advisor, etc., all in one business. Even if the financial advisor in the office has a solid record, you will want to double-check the experience and credentials of each professional to find out how successful they are in their area of expertise. In my experience, the best CPAs and estate planners have their own firms. You'll want to be sure you're getting the "best in breed" of all these professionals. All too often, we find that these "comprehensive" offices may have one or two experienced principal professionals, but beware; check that the "tax professional" or "estate attorney" has some experience and isn't just someone's nephew who just passed the bar or received their certificate and needed a job.

Breaking Up with Your Accumulation Advisor

To borrow from the immortal lyrics of Neil Sedaka, "Breaking up is hard to do." If you are at or nearing retirement, and you have an accumulation advisor whose dialogue no longer makes good investing sense to you, it's time to break up.

What's especially difficult is when you are going steady with your financial advisor all through your working years. But look at it this way—you no longer see a pediatrician when you reach adulthood, and you don't consult your podiatrist for dental work. We understand perfectly well when it's time to change doctors through the different stages of life or when we experience an issue with our health. It's much the same when dealing with wealth issues. Just as doctors have their own areas of expertise, so do financial advisors. Whether they deal in risk or safety is something you must determine for yourself.

What if your advisor is your best friend? Well, I must admit—that is a tough one. It becomes a personal issue. You don't want to risk losing a good friend. On the other hand, you probably don't want to risk losing your money in retirement, either. So, it may come down to how much that friendship is worth in terms of dollars and cents. I do know some retirees who allowed their portfolios to continue to underperform for years because they didn't want to hurt anyone's feelings. But I've known others who concluded that if the friendship hinged on continuing a business relationship that was no longer mutually beneficial, then it was probably a shallow friendship to begin with. In the end, it's a personal decision.

> "You just slip out the back, Jack
> Make a new plan, Stan
> You don't need to be coy, Roy
> Just get yourself free
> Hop on the bus, Gus
> You don't need to discuss much
> Just drop off the key, Lee
> And get yourself free"
> ~Paul Simon, American singer/songwriter
> *50 Ways to Leave Your Lover*

The transition from one advisor to another can be made with a simple phone call, email, or letter. Know when it is time to move on and recognize the importance of your financial future.

Summary

As you begin your journey down the path to financial security and independence, I want to leave you with this. I once met a successful business consultant who owned several businesses across the country—achieving wealth most of us can only dream of. He asked me what my number was. I had never been asked that question. I just tried to succeed and save the best way I thought I could. I realized I never really put a retirement plan together for myself to ultimately determine what number it was that I had to save to retire, and not just retire but feel financially free or Job Optional.

He said, "Once you reach that number, you will be amazed by the success you will achieve and the impact you make." It was enlightening, really. We are trained to think that getting to that number IS success. He said, "When you get there, you will begin to treat your business, family, clients, friends and yourself differently." At some point, when it's no longer about the money, you can change the world, leveraging your life savings to spend more time focusing on your unique purpose and delivering more meaning into your life.

For me, I have been so unbelievably blessed—lucky, some might say—that I am just getting there in my financial life. I'm beginning to see what he really meant, as it has changed all aspects of my life. Our business has begun to truly explode. We are able to give more back to our clients and provide services many financial firms simply won't because it's too expensive. We've lowered costs, undercutting other financial firms that are too driven by the bottom line. We also spend more time with our clients and prospective clients than other firms are willing to, as they are more worried about closing the next person walking through the door. We have the best staff we could ever imagine—providing better benefits and pay than our competitors, which in turn directly impacts the experience of the clients who choose to work with us.

In my personal life, I found ways to hire managers and staff to allow me to spend more time with my family than ever before. For years, I was in the office before the light came up and left after the sun went down seven days a week. When I first started working with my dad, I remember him picking me up at five in the morning and not getting home until midnight. Now, I get to take my kids out to the park during the week, get involved in church activities and have relationship-building getaways that have brought my wife and me closer than ever before—building the rock-solid marriage we've always wanted. It all started with the implementation of my very own Retire With Purpose™ Framework, allowing me to live the "Job Optional" lifestyle. I no longer worry about money, use net worth as a scorecard or concern myself with what happens in the next election or next year in the stock market. I focus on what matters, and it's not money. The same can be true for you.

Regardless of your life stage, you can get there. I've seen people who were already there and didn't know they were. Once a real retirement plan illustrated that they MADE IT, it allowed them to live like they never thought they could. They spent more time with family, doing recreational activities they lost touch with and even started second careers that fulfilled their dreams. The sooner you get started, the sooner you will get there.

Once you do, you will achieve levels of success in life you never thought possible. Here's to achieving financial independence and living your true PURPOSE, which I promise has nothing to do with money in the end.

TAKEAWAYS, ACTIONS AND NOTES

What are your biggest takeaways from this chapter?

_____
_____
_____
_____
_____
_____
_____

What are three action steps that you should work on now?

1. _____
2. _____
3. _____

What are three action steps for later?

1. _____
2. _____
3. _____

CLOSING

NOTES:

ABOUT THE AUTHOR

A fulfilling life begins with pinpointing your purpose. Casey Weade, Founder and CEO of Howard Bailey Financial, learned this firsthand when he achieved financial independence in his late twenties, unsure of how to leverage his newfound financial freedom. With his focus no longer needing to be on money, his mindset on his entire life path shifted.

"That was the moment I realized all of my goals had always been about the collection of money and things," Weade said. "They were void of those most meaningful moments in life."

For Weade, those moments included time spent with family, being present with his wife and kids and serving the community. He considered what it might look like to take early retirement, but that didn't fulfill his purpose. He reflected on his "why." Weade knew his purpose was to serve others and discovered there was a way he could continue to positively impact others.

"I realized that giving back doesn't mean you're just giving money away to charity," Weade said. "You can be most effective by utilizing those gifts you have. For me, that was finance: getting money, making money, investing, financial planning and goal setting. I uncovered a framework that I used in my own financial life, and without even really thinking about it, I structured a framework that delivered this financial freedom."

Weade developed the Howard Bailey propriety planning process, known as the Retire With Purpose™ Framework. This framework is rooted in Casey's belief that all retirement plans should be driven by meaning and purpose because, without purpose, we lack direction.

Alongside the Howard Bailey team, Casey is on a mission to help others gain clarity in purpose and elevate meaning in their lives through personal and practical financial strategies. He hosts the weekly *Retire With Purpose*™ radio show, which airs across the Midwest, as well as the national *Retire With Purpose*™ Podcast.

Casey is a Finance graduate of Stetson University. He is also a CERTIFIED FINANCIAL PLANNER™ (CFP®), Retirement Income Certified Professional® (RICP®), Chartered Life Underwriter® (CLU®) and Chartered Financial Consultant® (ChFC®). In addition, he is an Investment Advisor Representative (IAR), is licensed in life, accident and health insurance and is also Long-Term Care Certified.

Casey is a lifelong Midwest native and currently resides in Fort Wayne, Indiana, with his wife and three children. He sponsors the Howard Bailey Junior Golf Tour as part of the Indiana Golf Foundation and continues to stay active in his own community by supporting small businesses, local organizations and charities throughout the year.

More information on Casey can be found at HOWARDBAILEY.COM.

ACKNOWLEDGMENTS

Hundreds of hours have been poured into the content and development of what you just read. While I would like to take full credit for everything that has gone into this book, the reality is that it would not have come to fruition without the support of hundreds of individuals in my life.

First, I would like to thank all the families and friends who have put their trust and faith in our organization as the quarterbacks of their financial lives. I hope they have learned as much from me as I have learned from them over the many years they have been working with our team. I have learned about marriage, friendship, business and many more pieces of existential wisdom that I will pass on to as many people as I possibly can. My team and I could not have gotten where we are today without your support. And, to one of the first potential clients I ever met who told me I would not be a success in the business of financial planning until I was old and gray—thanks for giving me the motivation to persevere.

I could have never achieved an ounce of what I have to this day without the loving support of my wife, Chelsie. Since the day we met, she has patiently put up with the long hours I have put in growing the business we are so proud of, not to mention the time away I spent writing this book. Not only has she endured and encouraged the time I have devoted to our clients and business, but she herself has made this business a passion of her own. To share a passion with a spouse is a priceless commodity for which I will be forever grateful.

Chelsie has blessed me with three beautiful children, Calvin, Carver and Chloe. These three have taught me more than I would ever have imagined. Calvin always lightens the mood, letting me reflect on the simpler things in life. Carver illustrates to me that, no matter how small we are, we can overcome any obstacle. Chloe has shown me what true courage looks like and the power of adoption.

Obviously, none of this would be possible without the help of my parents bringing me into this world. My dad, Ron, has taught me the ropes and principles of finance starting at a very early age. He showed me how to be humble, curious, and driven to help others. My mom, Diann, imparted to me the importance of education, caring for others and giving back. She illustrated to me through her actions how to always be there to support others, just as she has been for me my entire life.

I would be remiss to leave out the team at Howard Bailey Financial, Inc. Our advisory team has shown me there are many financial planners out there today who are ready and willing to put their heart and soul into the selfless relationships they build with others every day. Many thanks to our staff for putting up with my constant energy and demands as we continue to see massive growth that couldn't be managed without their help. My eternal appreciation is due to the entire team at Howard Bailey for their love and commitment to the families we work with and for embracing our philosophy of always doing the BEST thing.

WHO IS HOWARD BAILEY?

There truly is no Howard Bailey that we know of. The company name was created by Casey in honor of his two biggest childhood mentors. Together, their names represent the values and philosophy the company was founded upon, not to mention shaping him into the man he is today.

Howard Weade is the grandfather of Casey Weade on his father's side. Howard lent much to the conservative investment approach ingrained in the mind of Casey, as well as the approach the Howard Bailey team utilizes today. When Casey asked his father, Ron Weade, what Howard was best at, he said saving. Ron was no different outside of his innate ability to connect and create lasting friendships.

Ralph **Bailey** is the grandfather of Casey Weade on his mother's side. Ralph's background in the local school system influenced the mentality Howard Bailey upholds these principles every day: focusing on educating clients and treating each as an individual. Ralph, like his daughter Diann Weade, Casey's mother, kept a steady focus on serving others and giving back.

Casey has strived to combine the attributes of his family in good financial stewardship as well as giving and serving others in his daily life and that of the company he founded, Howard Bailey.

HOWARD AND CHRISTINE WEADE

RALPH AND LORETTA BAILEY (WITH CASEY WEADE)

A BACKGROUND ON HOWARD BAILEY

Founded by Casey Weade in 2011, Howard Bailey provides comprehensive financial planning strategies to pre-retired and retired individuals across the country. The Howard Bailey team focuses on helping individuals achieve total wealth optimization and reliable income sources in retirement, all the while zoning in on their "why." The team at Howard Bailey believes money should deliver meaning AND purpose. Focusing on establishing a clear purpose for an individual's financial future, Casey and his team offer their proprietary planning Retire With Purpose™ Framework for identifying and most efficiently helping to defend against the biggest obstacles to one's financial freedom, allowing their clients to focus on their unique purpose and ultimately deliver more meaning to their lives.

For more information on how Casey and his team can help you achieve your Job Optional* retirement, visit www.howardbailey.com or call (866) 482-9559.

ENDNOTES

1) Asset allocation does not guarantee a profit or protect against a loss in a declining market. It is a method used to help manage investment risk.

2) Fixed annuities are long-term insurance contracts, and there is generally a surrender charge imposed during the first five to seven years that you own the annuity contract. Withdrawals prior to age fifty-nine-and-one-half may result in a 10 percent IRS tax penalty, in addition to any ordinary income tax. Any guarantees of the annuity are backed by the financial strength of the underlying insurance company.

3) Dollar-cost averaging may help reduce per share cost through continuous investment in securities regardless of fluctuating prices and does not guarantee profitability nor can it protect from loss in a declining market. The investor should consider his/her ability to continue investing through periods of low price levels.

4) Raymond Fazzi. FA Financial Advisor. February 7, 2018. "Edelman: Retirement Models Seriously Flawed; Age Projections

Should Be To 120." https://www.fa-mag.com/news/edelman-says-retirement-planning-should-project-to-age-120-37038.html

5) U.S. Department of Health and Human Services. April 27, 2022. "Aging." https://www.hhs.gov/aging/index.html

6) J.P. Morgan Asset Management. "Guide to Retirement" https://am.jpmorgan.com/us/en/asset-management/adv/insights/retirement-insights/guide-to-retirement/

7) Greg Iacurci. CNBC. May 11, 2022. "How fast does inflation cut buying power? Here's a simple guide." https://www.cnbc.com/2022/05/11/how-fast-does-inflation-cut-buying-power-heres-a-simple-guide.html

8) Exchange-traded funds (ETFs) are sold by prospectus. Please consider the investment objectives, risks, charges, and expenses carefully before investing. The prospectus, which contains this and other information about the investment company, can be obtained from the fund company or your financial professional. Be sure to read the prospectus carefully before deciding whether to invest.

9) Selena Maranjian. The Motley Fool. August 12, 2023. "Will the 4% Rule for Retirement Withdrawals Leave You Broke?" https://www.fool.com/retirement/2023/08/12/will-the-4-rule-for-retirement-withdrawals-leave-y/

10) Alana Benson. Nerdwallet. October 24, 2023. "What Is the Average Retirement Savings by Age?" https://www.nerdwallet.com/article/investing/the-average-retirement-savings-by-age-and-why-you-need-more

11) Maurie Backman. The Motley Fool. July 7, 2023. "This Is the Average Income for Retirees in America" https://www.fool.com/research/average-retirement-income/

ENDNOTES

12) Guarantees provided are based on the claims-paying ability of the issuing company.

13) FDIC. March 20, 2023. "Deposit Insurance FAQs." https://www.fdic.gov/resources/deposit-insurance/faq/

14) Board of Governors of the Federal Reserve System. January 4, 2022. "Reserve Requirements" https://www.federalreserve.gov/monetarypolicy/reservereq.htm.

15) Board of Governors of the Federal Reserve System. January 4, 2022. "Reserve Requirements" https://www.federalreserve.gov/monetarypolicy/reservereq.htm

16) Practicing Law Institute. "Insurance Regulation Answer Book (2020 Edition)" https://www.pli.edu/catalog/publications/answer-book/insurance-regulation-answer-book

17) Elisabeth Buchwald. CNN Business. May 1, 2023. "As PacWest shares dive, are we seeing the 2008 financial crisis all over again?" https://www.cnn.com/2023/05/11/business/2008-banking-crisis-comparison/index.html

18) Robert C. Merton. Harvard Business Review. July-August 2014. "The Crisis in Retirement Planning." https://hbr.org/2014/07/the-crisis-in-retirement-planning

19) Indexed annuities are insurance contracts that, depending on the contract, may offer a guaranteed annual interest rate and some participation growth, if any, of a stock market index. Such contracts have substantial variation in terms, costs of guarantees and features, and may cap participation or returns in significant ways. Any guarantees offered are backed by the financial strength of the insurance company. Surrender charges apply if not held to the end of the term. Withdrawals are taxed as ordinary income and, if taken prior to fifty-nine-and-one-half, a 10 percent federal tax penalty. Investors

are cautioned to carefully review an indexed annuity for its features, costs, risks, and how the variables are calculated.

20) Indices are unmanaged, and investors cannot invest directly in an index. Unless otherwise noted, the performance of indices does not account for any fees, commissions, or other expenses that would be incurred. Returns do not include reinvested dividends.

The Standard & Poor's 500 (S&P 500) is an unmanaged group of securities considered to be representative of the stock market in general. It is a market-value-weighted index with each stock's weight in the index proportionate to its market value.

21) Allianz. "Understanding fixed index annuities" https://www.allianzlife.com/~/media/files/global/documents/2016/05/18/08/18/m-5217.pdf

This chart is a hypothetical representation of fixed index annuity growth of $100k under varying market/index conditions and is not meant to represent the performance of any specific product. The black line shows the S&P® 500 annual return rate from 2000-2017, according to data from Yahoo Finance (https://yhoo.it/2SJ61Bm). The grey line shows the annual point-to-point strategy with 50 percent market participation. Participation rates are usually found in point-to-point indexing strategies. The higher the participation rate, the more interest you will be credited with when the market index (S&P® 500, for example) is moving up. Let's say that you were offered an uncapped, point-to-point account with a 50 percent participation rate. If the chosen index increased by 10 percent, then you would receive 50 percent of the gain or a 5 percent rate of return on your money that year. If the S&P® had a negative return, then zero interest would be credited to the fixed index annuity.

22) Riders are available for an additional fee—some riders may not be available in all states.

ENDNOTES

23) Please consider the investment objectives, risks, charges, and expenses carefully before investing in variable annuities. The prospectus, which contains this and other information about the variable annuity contract and the underlying investment options, can be obtained from the insurance company or your financial professional. Be sure to read the prospectus carefully before deciding whether to invest.

The investment return and principal value of the variable annuity investment options are not guaranteed. Variable annuity sub-accounts fluctuate with changes in market conditions. The principal may be worth more or less than the original amount invested when the annuity is surrendered.

24) https://retirewithpurpose.com/podcast/011-rethinking-reverse-mortgages-and-building-better-portfolios-with-dr-wade-pfau/

25) Roger Ibbotson. Zebra. January, 2018. "Fixed Indexed Annuities: Consider the Alternative" https://www.zebracapital.com/wp-content/uploads/2019/06/Fixed-Indexed-Annuities-Consider-the-Alternative-January-2018.pdf

26) Not associated with or endorsed by the Social Security Administration or any other government agency.

27) Erin Oppenheim. Nerdwallet. August 25, 2023. "Is There a Social Security Spousal Benefits Loophole?" https://www.ncrdwallet.com/article/investing/social-security/spousal-benefits-loophole

28) Social Security Matters. August 24, 2023. "Do You Qualify for Social Security Spouse's Benefits?" https://blog.ssa.gov/do-you-qualify-for-social-security-spouses-benefits/

29) Social Security Administration. "If You Are the Survivor" https://www.ssa.gov/benefits/survivors/ifyou.html

30) ssa.gov. 2021. Retirement Benefits: Income Taxes And Your Social Security Benefit. https://www.ssa.gov/benefits/retirement/planner/taxes.html

31) Roberta Pescow. Nerdwallet. June 7, 2023. "What Is the 2023 Medicare IRMAA, and When Does It Apply?" https://www.nerdwallet.com/article/insurance/medicare/what-is-the-medicare-irmaa

32) Evan T. Beach. Kiplinger. June 1, 2023. "Which Retirement Accounts Should You Withdraw From First?" https://www.kiplinger.com/retirement/which-retirement-accounts-to-withdraw-from-first

33) Erica Lamberg. Fox Business. June 25, 2023. "Inside America's retirement income crisis." https://www.foxbusiness.com/markets/inside-americas-retirement-income-crisis

34) Based on data from Blanchett, David. 2014. "Exploring the Retirement Consumption Puzzle." Journal of Financial Planning 27 (5): 34-42

35) Susann Rohwedder, Michael D. Hurd, and Péter Hudomiet. Michigan Retirement and Disability Research Center. June 2022. "Explanations for the Decline in Spending at Older Ages." https://mrdrc.isr.umich.edu/publications/papers/pdf/wp440.pdf

36) Wayne Duggan. Forbes Advisor. May 4, 2023. "Is Gold An Inflation Hedge?" https://www.forbes.com/advisor/investing/gold-inflation-hedge/

37) Mia Huang. Dimensional. April 5, 2022. "Should You Chase Dividend Stocks to Combat Inflation and Rate Hikes?" https://www.dimensional.com/gb-en/insights/should-you-chase-dividend-stocks-to-combat-inflation-and-rate-hikes

38) Jessica Bebel. Morningstar. June 16, 2023. "Are Stocks a Good Hedge Against Inflation?" https://www.morningstar.com/financial-advice/are-stocks-good-inflation-hedges

ENDNOTES

39) Kristina Zucchi. Investopedia. August 29, 2023. "Inflation's Impact on Stock Returns." https://www.investopedia.com/articles/investing/052913/inflations-impact-stock-returns.asp

40) Roger Ibbotson. Zebra. January, 2018. "Fixed Indexed Annuities: Consider the Alternative" https://www.zebracapital.com/wp-content/uploads/2019/06/Fixed-Indexed-Annuities-Consider-the-Alternative-January-2018.pdf

41) TreasuryDirect. "Treasury Inflation Protected Securities (TIPS)" https://www.treasurydirect.gov/marketable-securities/tips/

42) GAO. July 27, 2021. "401(k) Retirement Plans: Many Participants Do Not Understand Fee Information, but DOL Could Take Additional Steps to Help Them" https://www.gao.gov/products/gao-21-357

43) Kevin Voigt. Nerdwallet. February 2, 2023. "Mutual Fund Fees: A Guide for Beginners" https://www.nerdwallet.com/article/investing/mutual-fund-fees-what-investors-need-to-know

44) Christine Benz. Morningstar. June 30, 2023. "Which Investments to Keep Out of Your Taxable Account" https://www.morningstar.com/personal-finance/which-investments-keep-out-your-taxable-account

45) Barbara Marquand. Nerdwallet. July 7, 2023. "Long-Term Care Insurance Explained." https://www.nerdwallet.com/article/insurance/long-term-care-insurance

Shawn Plummer. annuityexpertadvice.com. 2023. "What Is A Nursing Home?" https://www.annuityexpertadvice.com/nursing-home/

46) Genworth Financial. 2021. "Cost of Care Survey" https://www.genworth.com/about-us/industry-expertise/cost-of-care.html

47) IRS. Dec. 9, 2022. "Retirement Topics - Beneficiary." https://www.irs.gov/retirement-plans/plan-participant-employee/retirement-topics-beneficiary

48) Dayana Yochim. Nerdwallet. July 14, 2023. "Index Funds vs. Mutual Funds: The Differences That Matter." https://www.nerdwallet.com/article/investing/index-funds-vs-mutual-funds

49) IRS. August 29, 2023. "IRA FAQs - Distributions (Withdrawals)" https://www.irs.gov/retirement-plans/retirement-plans-faqs-regarding-iras-distributions-withdrawals

50) For more information, read my article in Kiplinger's: https://www.kiplinger.com/article/investing/T023-C032-S014-don-t-be-fooled-by-impressive-financial-credential.html

51) Zippia Team. Zippia. November 15, 2022. "WHY I QUIT BEING A FINANCIAL ADVISOR?" https://www.zippia.com/answers/why-i-quit-being-a-financial-advisor/

52) https://www.azlyrics.com/lyrics/paulsimon/50waystoleaveyourlover.html Paul Simon lyrics are the property and copyright of their owners. "50 Ways to Leave Your Lover" lyrics are provided for educational purposes and personal use only.